BEYOND E[...]

Doddy Hay is well quali[...] [...]
under stress: teacher, tai[l gunner?], [test] parachut-
ist and international sky-diver, county cricketer
and inter-Service rugby footballer, competitive
rider on the Cresta Run, regular officer and
irregular broadcaster, syndicated sports writer
and author of books about test flyers, bullfighters
and merchant seamen at war, he has spent most
of his life where the action is. It is the insight
gained from these experiences that he brings to
bear upon the two heroes of this book, upon the
hostile interdependence of two men flung without warning into a situation of desperate danger
that came close to killing them both but, in the
event, taught them and us all something about
the nature of man when stripped to the
essentials.

Doddy Hay lives in Fife, Scotland.

Also by the same author:

Your Guide to Norway (Alvin Redman, 1967)
Hit the Silk (Heinemann, 1968)
The Man in the Hot Seat (Collins, Reader's Digest, 1969)
The Bullfight (New English Library, 1976)
War Under the Red Ensign (Jane's, 1982)

DODDY HAY

Beyond Endurance

FONTANA/Collins

First published in 1989 by Fontana Paperbacks
8 Grafton Street, London W1X 3LA

Copyright © Doddy Hay, 1989

Printed and bound in Great Britain by
William Collins Sons & Co. Ltd, Glasgow

CONDITIONS OF SALE
This book is sold subject to the condition that
it shall not, by way of trade or otherwise, be
lent, re-sold, hired out or otherwise circulated
without the publisher's prior consent in any
form of binding or cover other than that
in which it is published and without a similar
condition including this condition being
imposed on the subsequent purchaser.

CONTENTS

Dedication vi
Acknowledgements vii
Preface viii
Beyond Endurance 1
Appendix I 159
Appendix II 171
Appendix III 179

DEDICATION

It was never our intention to tell anyone the story of what happened on board the raft or what we went through. The disaster which resulted in the loss of our crewmates was, we felt, a personal tragedy to be suffered alone. That is until Mr José Delgado and his brother Felipe came to our homes one day and pleaded with us to speak of our ordeal, which, they said, ought not to remain for ever concealed in the dark shadows of our minds but should be made public for the benefit of humanity. We therefore agreed and have now related the most significant events of that fateful voyage with the sole aim of contributing to any recommendations or conclusions which may be drawn from our bitter experience.

We apologize most sincerely to the relatives of our late shipmates for having taken the liberty of mentioning some of their names, but we had to stick to the facts and that is the policy we have adhered to throughout the narrative.

This book is dedicated to the memory of our lamented companions who went down with the *Berge Istra* – from Captain Kristoffer Hemnes to the last crewmember, and to their bereaved families.

IMELDO AND EPIFANIO

ACKNOWLEDGEMENTS

There are many people and institutions whose help was invaluable in collecting the facts upon which this book is based. Mr Gordon Evans for his overall technical research; Miss Anne Cowne, Lloyd's shipping registry, London; Mr R. A. Keene, Lloyd's of London; Mr Machardy, British Petroleum (Shipping) Ltd; Surgeon Commander Frank Golden, Institute of Naval Medicine (Portsmouth); Mr D. B. Foy; Mr Makio Ino, Japanese Maritime Safety Agency, Tokyo; Mr José O. de Gomez, PAGASA Manilla, Philippines; Mr Pharance, *Daily Telegraph*, London; The National Maritime Museum, Greenwich, London; The Climatology Department of the Meteorological Office, Bracknell, Berkshire; The Office of the Hidrographer of the Navy, Taunton, Somerset; J. D. Potter Ltd, London; The Admiralty Library, Fulham, London; Decca Navigation, London; The 18th Tactical Fighter Wing USAF, Kadena, Japan; Mr Ketteridge, Department of Trade and Industry, London; Mr Barry Shapcott, London; Master Sergeant John E. Reinders, 18th Tactical Fighter Wing, USAF, San Francisco; Juan Pedro Valdes, photographer, Tenerife; Rafael Valenciano, Tenerife; Juan A. Padron Albornoz.

PREFACE

My interest in the loss and disappearance of the supertanker *Berge Istra* and in the ordeal suffered by her two survivors was first aroused in the summer of 1982, when I was introduced to Señor José Delgado, to whom this book is dedicated, and without whom it would not and could not have been written.

I had spent the previous two years researching and writing a book about the British Merchant Navy at war, *War Under the Red Ensign* (Jane's, 1982), and, although my own military experience had been gained in the air, I was, in 1982, very deeply aware of and concerned about the dangers of the sea. For many months past I had lived amongst seamen, researching my book, had spent my working and my leisure time, which had been virtually indivisible, almost exclusively in their company. By courtesy of the National Union of Seamen I had occupied first an apartment in their headquarters, Maritime House in Clapham, and later a room at Springbok-Radcliffe Farm in Surrey, a rest and retirement home for men of the Merchant Navy. In both I had spent my time, day and night, shamelessly begging for anecdotes and reminiscences to illustrate what life at sea is really all about, and seamen of vast experience had come forward in their willing dozens to paint for me the picture I was seeking.

I spent long hours in the reading room of the Imperial War Museum, and one marvellous and memorable weekend as a guest at the biennial reunion in Plymouth of Merchant Navy ex-prisoners of war, a weekend where the talks lasted far into the night and the stories were true tales of hardship, courage, and almost unbelievable endurance. In response to my appeals in the press and on both radio and television, countless other survivors of the war at sea – and in several cases, relatives of some who had *not* survived – had entered into correspondence with me that lasted for many months and enabled me to fill several box-files with detailed and often harrowing accounts of what shipwreck and abandonment can mean to those who suffer it.

More than that: to provide an epilogue to *War Under the Red Ensign* I had travelled to Soviet Russia to see for myself the 'other' end of the run on these appalling arctic convoys, and to meet, in Moscow, Murmansk and Archangel, men and women who travelled from all over the Soviet Union to recall for my benefit their own often dreadful memories of these desperate, dangerous days. They came from all levels of society, these veterans: I met dockers and crane drivers, air marshals, bosuns and generals, and I had the first interview granted in years by the octogenarian Admiral Ivan Papanin, twice made Hero of the Soviet Union, a sailor, scientist and explorer who charted and opened up the waters of the Arctic. In short, by the time *War Under the Red Ensign* had been published, I felt I had absorbed some valuable understanding of disaster at sea.

It was his awareness of this that induced Gordon Evans, a professional maritime researcher who had helped me in seeking out information from the wartime archives, to suggest that I now consider a project in which he himself had been engaged but which had been abandoned several years previously as impracticable. He showed me several bulky files of correspondence, pictures, technical data, diary notes and transcriptions from the tapes of some thirty hours of recorded conversation with the protagonists of the story. Naturally I was puzzled as to why such a wealth of research material, most of it gathered by Mr Evans himself, had been allowed to lie for so many months in desuetude.

The explanation was strange, and sad but simple. The private investigation into the sinking of the *Berge Istra* had been initiated by Señor Delgado as a form of occupational therapy following a personal bereavement, and as such it had already served its purpose. The original intention had been first to unearth and later to tell the story of Imeldo Barreto Léon and Epifanio Perdomo López, and to explain why these two men had adamantly refused to talk publicly in any detail about their horrendous experiences, adrift for nearly three weeks on a tiny, broken raft in the South Pacific Ocean. This intention had been achieved only in part: Señor Delgado and Mr Evans between them had collected and collated a great mass of information on every aspect of the *Berge Istra* disaster – but they had *not*, since neither of them is nor aspires to be a professional writer, succeeded in sifting and transcribing this research material into a narrative that could even be considered for publication.

This was the essential point in the provenance of the present volume, and it may be relevant here to mention certain circumstances that could have influenced Señor Delgado, on meeting me to discuss the project, to hand into my keeping all the research material, with the exclusive right to use it as the basis of a book if such seemed practicable. Reference has already been made to *War Under the Red Ensign*, but that was not the first book I had published that related to the problems and the attitudes of men under stress. Drawing upon personal experience of both military and experimental aviation I had written a successful book about the true nature of test flying and of the men who engage in it, *The Man in the Hot Seat* (Collins, 1969). Further, while living for more than a decade in Spain, I had followed for years the phenomenon of the *fiesta brava*, had travelled with *toreros*, talked in depth with many of them before and after their encounters in the arena, and had subsequently published what amounted to a survey of the whole history of the bull fight and of the men who risk their lives daily to engage in it, *The Bullfight* (New English Library, 1976). The above activities, like those of the men of the Merchant Navy, expose for examination men's reaction to stress and danger – and that, rather than the sinking of a huge and seemingly unsinkable vessel, is what this story is all about.

DODDY HAY
Fife, November 1989

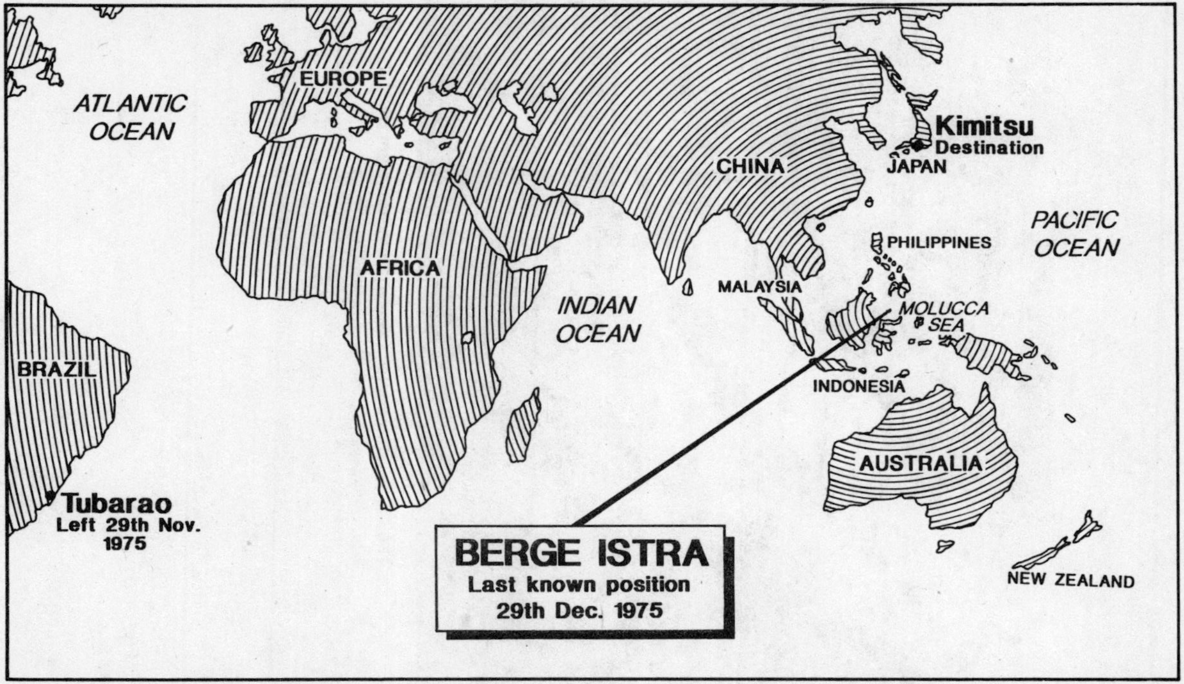
ATLANTIC OCEAN
EUROPE
AFRICA
BRAZIL
Tubarao
Left 29th Nov. 1975
CHINA
Kimitsu
Destination
JAPAN
PACIFIC OCEAN
PHILIPPINES
MALAYSIA
INDIAN OCEAN
MOLUCCA SEA
INDONESIA
AUSTRALIA
NEW ZEALAND
BERGE ISTRA
Last known position
29th Dec. 1975

The *Berge Istra,* copied from a photograph lent by
kind permission of the Bergesen DY Group

Chapter One

ON TUESDAY 30 DECEMBER 1975, at half past four on an afternoon of blistering sunshine, Imeldo Barreto Léon found himself alone and dying in the middle of the Molucca Sea, somewhere between Tubarao in Brazil, and Kimitsu in Japan. He was dying because he was drowning and choking in a vast, shimmering cauldron of oil; he was alone because in a few horrendous seconds his personal world and its other inhabitants had totally disappeared.

It took time and an agonizing journey backwards through bewilderment to bring him to accept that where he was and what had happened was reality and not the chimera of some surrealistic nightmare: that one of the biggest ships in the world was no longer afloat, that nothing, *nothing* was visible for miles around him, except a few pieces of fabric and shattered furniture bobbing listlessly on a sullen, heaving carpet of black, glistening oil.

His first real memory, from only seconds before, was of a frenzied battle to reach the unseen surface, of the crushing pressure which seemed to cave his head inwards, and of the growing hallucination that he was already dead, a fancy dispelled only by the searing pain in his bursting and polluted lungs as he had struggled towards daylight and air. A thousand speculations remained unanswered, but he knew that at least he was alive, and only one question was of true importance — for how long?

Dog-paddling desperately with one hand as he raked cloying filth from his eyes and mouth with the other, he forced himself to concentrate, to identify and evaluate the wreckage floating around him, and at last he saw what he was praying for, a life-raft slipping and sliding across his line of vision only twenty yards away. *Only?* His arms and legs felt as if they had been wrenched from their sockets, his head was a hammering drum of terror and confusion, and it took an almost superhuman effort of will to drag himself across that seemingly interminable gap towards at least temporary survival.

The raft, when at last he reached it, made a sorry haven: a shallow polystyrene mattress broken in the middle, its inboard length was less than that of his own body. But it bore his weight; shell-shocked and spent from his efforts, Imeldo Barreto Léon nonetheless was floating, and he was alive.

The future could wait. First, for the sake of his sanity, he must somehow piece together the events leading up to the instantaneous destruction and complete disappearance of the supertanker *Berge Istra*, a vessel almost three times the length of a football stadium, with a displacement five times that of the Titanic. Imeldo's mind raced on. The explosions, three of them in rapid succession: thundering blasts that had lifted nearby men off their feet and left them – he could swear it – hovering in the shaking air several inches above the deck. The deck itself, hundreds of yards of plated steel, ripped open like a sardine can, the great gouts of smoke and flame engulfing the superstructure and the bridge. Then there was the awesome lurch to port that had sent the huge ship, over a quarter of a million tons of her, canting over on her side like a dinghy in a squall.

Now think, man, think – what was happening before all that?

We were working, of course – what else? In heat, real heat, heat so bad it scorched our feet through the inch-thick rubber soles of our sandals. I was with three others – José, Daniel, and Manuel – scraping the hatch-cover in front of Number 1 hold, preparing it for painting. But we weren't the only ones at work. On the way up to our station from the afternoon coffee break we'd passed the welder, busy on his knees between hatches 6, 7, and 8.

Then the bosun came by and told us we'd be doing two hours' overtime on another painting job. He took Manuel with him to collect the paint from the store, leaving the rest of us to clean up the deck and stow the tools. I started sweeping things clear with an air hose while the others picked up the gear to take it to the fo'c'sle.

Then came a rumbling, rushing sound followed by the deafening bang of the first explosion. An enormous crack split clear across the main deck opposite tank Number 8, where the welder was working, and I saw him tossed high in the air as a sheet of flame spread across the bridge, so that everything abaft of it simply disappeared.

It was at this point that Imeldo's memory became less kaleidoscopic, recording events and impressions in their natural sequence. As he and the two men beside him made a dash for the ladder some twenty feet for'ard of them – a slippery, steel-runged pathway to the comparative safety of the fo'c'sle head – a second explosion ripped another huge hole in the tanker, and the seas, rushing in, thrust her still further over on to her port side. Until that moment Imeldo had been bravely hanging on to the air hose, afraid that if he released it the uncontrolled power would send the heavy metal nozzle snaking and flailing towards his companions. Now, as the air supply failed and the hose went dead, he threw it aside. He registered a sudden shout, a facial expression, a momentary tableau straight from the brush of Hieronymus Bosch that he would never forget.

José Ferrer Negrin, who at forty-eight was a shipmate of

long experience and almost a decade older than himself, stood clinging to a rail, staring at the gap where the bridge had been, his eyes and voice an unholy amalgam of terror, fury and above all pure hatred. He was screaming at his dead officers, 'Now, you bastards, you have it – there you have it, you bastards.' These were the last words Imeldo ever heard him speak.

The whole port side of the ship was now ablaze. Imeldo decided upon a headlong dash to starboard, where, high out of the water, one lifeboat still swung undamaged on its davits, when suddenly his arm was roughly grasped by another seaman shouting, 'No, no – we're going down. The rafts are nearer.'

Between them they struggled to unlash the nearest life-raft when there came the third and final explosion, the effect of which was beyond belief. It blew the *Berge Istra* apart and tossed it over in the water from its port to its starboard side. Over a quarter of a million tons of metal and ballast turned like an omelette in a pan . . . It also blew Imeldo Barreto Léon into the oblivion from which he was only now returning. That momentary hesitation, that other seaman's intervention, had unquestionably saved his life.

A brief inspection showed that the raft in which he now found himself, a flimsy structure at best, had been badly damaged. The sole protection it would have offered against the elements – a folding canopy supported by tubular struts – had been torn away in the blast, leaving four ugly screws projecting from the floor which destroyed any hope he might have had of achieving a position even remotely compatible with comfort. Its freeboard was a paltry eight inches, and the weight of Imeldo's body was enough to bring even the present calm seas disturbingly close to its upper rim.

Gazing around, he began to select treasures from such

flotsam as was within reach. First, a slat of broken furniture – that would certainly serve as a paddle. Next, two lifejackets, obviously of value both now and in such future as might lie ahead of him. A coil of rope – which, like the string he always carried in his boyhood pockets, was sure to come in handy sometime and might even serve as a drag-anchor should the sea turn rough. Best of all, a sheet of plastic – now that was a find indeed, blanket, awning, sunshade, umbrella, even – most vital of all to survival – a catchment container, should the good Lord send him rain.

His spirits rising, he began to believe for the first time that he might, after all, survive not only the sinking of his ship but also being adrift in mid-ocean. The sea was calm and smooth, the weather fine without a cloud in the sky, and surely soon – perhaps even now, if a distress signal had been sent out – help would be on its way. The loss of a property insured for thirteen million pounds, he reflected wryly, was not likely to pass unnoticed.

In the midst of this musing Imeldo made a further discovery, one that caused his throat to constrict and his heart to jump in sudden terror: he found that he was not, after all, alone. Alongside the raft a body, scarcely recognizable as such in the reeking filth around it, was wallowing face-downwards within inches of him, almost nudging the shallow platform on which he lay. That the man was dead he had no doubt, for there was no conscious movement and the face was buried deep in the sloughing oil. With his peasant's superstitions and innate horror of the dead, his first inclination was to thrust the body from him and to paddle away, eyes closed, from this grim reminder of the fate that had befallen his friends.

Decency, however, and perhaps even the wild hope that against all evidence the man might still be alive, won over his fear and repugnance, and, crouching over the rim of the raft, he wrapped both arms around the unmoving, oil-filmed chest and began to heave the floating body upright. It slipped and it slithered, and once or twice he almost lost it as the limp arms dropped forward from the shoulders, but finally he succeeded in dragging it over the gun'le. He released it thankfully and watched with vanishing hopes as it sprawled face down and lifeless on the narrow floor. And yet . . . With some rudimentary understanding of first aid he pressed rhythmically inwards and upwards on the waist and rib-cage, and was finally rewarded when some fragments of half-digested food came spewing out. Food – but no water; hope rekindled. Whatever disaster had struck this shipmate, he clearly had not drowned.

Turning the man's head sideways, and using one arm to lever the chest upwards, Imeldo bent his own face forward in an attempt to blow air into the lungs, but found at once that this was impossible. The tongue was curled and twisted, the mouth an evil-smelling mass of frothy spittle, oil, grease and ragged particles of meat and biscuit through which breath could never pass. With his fingers he gently straightened out the tongue and teased out what he could of the rubbish around it. Then, somehow forcing himself to conquer his nausea, he pressed his face forward once again and continued his efforts at mouth-to-mouth resuscitation. Several times disgust overwhelmed him and he himself was sick, yet he persisted, minute after minute, blowing, breathing, vomiting and then blowing again until at last the patient's belly began to quiver. The stomach distended, the navel popped outwards, and in a long series of trembling, writhing convulsions the body came dramatically back to life with the shuddering, wailing howl of a new-born child.

With cries of gratitude to his saints Imeldo rolled the man over on to his back. He dipped his hand in the sea and feverishly began to wipe the coated grease and vomit from the upturned face. As the man's features became recognizable, however, he recoiled with an involuntary gasp of horror at what he had just so painfully achieved. For the face staring wild-eyed up at him was that of the one man in all the world he most loathed and feared. It was the face of Epifanio Perdomo López, who was shunned and detested by each and every member of the *Berge Istra*'s crew. It was the face of a sullen, truculent, ill-natured man of dark moods who, only weeks before, had boasted of having served nine years in prison for the murder of a drinking companion in a dockside quarrel.

Chapter Two

IMELDO HAD A LIFETIME'S EXPERIENCE of the sea. Born into poverty at Icod de los Vinos, a pleasant old town of narrow winding streets on the island of Tenerife in the Canaries, he had been transported in infancy to the hamlet of Homician on the Punta de Hidalgo, a rocky headland on the island's northern shore. The son and grandson of fisherfolk, he had been brought up, like his six brothers, to earn his living from a small boat, and as a young boy had learned to assume the outlook and responsibilities of a man. He had seen his chance of a formal education disappear because of the need to contribute to the family income, and it was only as an adult that he had managed to teach himself to read and write. It was perhaps because of this that now, at the age of forty-one, his was a gentle, introspective personality, self-effacing and shy to the point of instinctive mistrustfulness. Bereft of the company of his wife and four children, whom he idolized, he was, in essence, a loner.

Although uneducated, he was not in any sense a stupid man. His natural response to problems great or small, however, was largely pragmatic, and was severely limited by his lack of worldly experience. Faced with an unfamiliar situation he would think things through logically enough, but would seldom come up with a decisive answer or a positive course of action. His reasoning was almost unbelievably simplistic; asked once what he considered the fundamental difference between men and women, he replied in all seriousness that women wore their hair long whereas men cut theirs short – a remark that in the mid-1970s made clear not only the naïvety of his outlook but also the limitations of his knowledge of the world at large. But Imeldo's simplicity was a good simplicity. He was a compassionate man who believed devoutly in God and in his family, and he was content in his beliefs.

Imeldo's compassionate nature was to be tried severely during the weeks to follow. Epifanio Perdomo López was not really a sailor at all, still less a seaman – not as these terms have been understood for centuries in Bristol or Nantucket. Born on the rugged Taganana Heights above Tenerife, he had been a builder's labourer, but the economic climate of the Canaries could be as harsh and unremitting as the long days of sunshine are balmy, and that was what had sent Epifanio to sea. He had responded not to the beckoning romance of a life on the ocean wave, but to the more prosaic attraction of a steady job with a relatively high wage earned in conditions where for weeks or months on end there would be neither need nor opportunity for any great personal expenditure.

In theory, admirable – but theory takes no account of the essential nature of the man, paradoxically sharp but shallow. Unlike Imeldo, he had attended school until the age of thirteen and had earned a certificate of education without undue difficulty, but his record thereafter was that of someone lacking in maturity. Now thirty-seven, Epifanio had married at twenty and seen the union run into almost immediate difficulty because of his stubborn refusal to accept any degree of domestic responsibility. Quick, bright, and even witty when in the right mood, he was both a drinker and a compulsive womanizer, and almost all his free time was devoted to the pursuit of both hobbies in the local *tavernas* – Almost all: he had spent sufficient time at home to sire nine children. But the home he had provided for these children, and for his wife, was a cave – literally a cave – in the mountains of Tenerife.

Here on the broken life-raft, however, it was not Epifanio's marital peccadilloes that struck terror in Imeldo's heart. His fear was of the darker side of Epifanio's disturbed and disturbing personality. The sheer unpredictability of the man, the constant uncertainty as to what sudden and seemingly unprovoked change of mood would come over him next, had frightened bigger and braver men than Imeldo. One moment he would be boasting extravagantly of wild adventures and imagined achievements, usually heroic; the next brooding bitterly over equally imaginary slights and grievances.

Hard enough to accept or even avoid aboard a vessel the size of a small village, this was the enforced companionship now facing Imeldo on a five-foot platform with nothing around them but the sea and the probability of a lonely, lingering death. Timid by nature, Imeldo shivered, but went silently on with the task of tending to Epifanio's wounds.

First, however, Imeldo did something that showed touching recognition of a man's need for dignity even in such desperate circumstances. The shock of the final explosion or the suction of the sinking had stripped Epifanio of virtually all his clothing. He now lay naked save only for his oil-soaked vest. Imeldo, before even searching the raft for the survival kit he knew must be somewhere to hand, removed his own trousers, peeled off his underpants and, by clothing Epifanio in them, helped restore to him some small semblance of normality and self-esteem.

Closer examination by Imeldo of his companion revealed a deep cut on Epifanio's head, another on one arm and, worst of all, severe and ugly gashes on both legs. He was clearly in great pain, and could hardly move his head or legs. In a compartment on one side of the raft Imeldo found a sealed plastic drum that provided his immediate requirements: first, a pair of surgical scissors with which he cut away the hair clotted around the headwound; next, a can of drinking water that he used willingly but unwisely to bathe the torn flesh. A moment's clear thinking, easy to write about but sometimes uncommonly hard to command, would have told him not only that fresh water was the most precious commodity they possessed, but also that sea water with its saline, antiseptic properties would have been the better dressing for the man's injuries. It was an error he was to regret bitterly in the days ahead.

Epifanio's behaviour after his wounds had been superficially cleaned might initially have been regarded charitably and even with sympathy – the man was, after all, both in pain and in shock. But moaning lamentations and self-pity can be tolerated for just so long by one who is himself shocked, terrified, and in the same mortal danger. Eventually Imeldo, ignoring his companion's demands for constant attention, busied himself in a detailed survey of what weapons were available to them in the forthcoming battle for survival. It took no great time to list them. The raft had two emergency compartments, one on each side, and between them they yielded up: five packets of vitamin biscuits, sixteen half-litre cans of water, five bottles of medicinal pills, three rolls of sticking-plaster, eight syringes of penicillin, one torch, four batteries, one pair of surgical scissors, four rolls of antiseptic gauze, one clasp-knife/tin opener, two red dishcloths, two strips of suppositories, two orange inflatable lifejackets, one baling scoop, two four-inch sponges, one pocket mirror, four signal flares, one packet of fish hooks, one landing-net.

As they glumly considered these items, the one thought

uppermost in each man's mind was that they might yet, in the oil and debris around them, find some other shipmates who had, against all the odds, survived the disaster. But soon even this faint hope became tainted by a fear that grew steadily inside them. With Epifanio lying injured and Imeldo crouched precariously beside him, they had no effective control over the drifting of the raft and were committed inexorably to travelling at whatever speed and in whatever direction the wind and current might carry them. As the implications of this began to sink in, the hope that they might find one or more of their friends among the flotsam gave way to something very close to a prayer that they should do no such thing. For it would be more than they could endure to come across such a man, perhaps even see him waving or calling out thankfully to them, and to know that if he were beyond their immediate reach there would be not one single thing they could do to save him.

The swift fall of darkness put an end to such morbid speculation, for all likelihood of finding other survivors died with the daylight. In its place, however, came an increasing awareness, no longer shrouded in shock, of the magnitude of the *Berge Istra* tragedy, and of the stark realities of their first night afloat on the raft. For a time Imeldo, his thoughts full of his lost friends and of his family, simply sat and wept silently, while Epifanio kept up his endless litany of complaint. How could God – or for that matter, Imeldo – expect him to lie here with his open wounds in this loathsome stew of oil and water, grease and blood slopping queasily back and forth with every movement of their little platform? How could he, Epifanio, be asked to endure such torment when every cautious attempt to find a position of some comfort merely added to the pain?

Imeldo's response was both patient and practical. With the scoop from the survival kit he began baling out, his rhythmic, sweeping movements accompanied by forced words of hope and encouragement. 'By tomorrow, every ship on this ocean will be looking for us.

'The Radio Officer must have managed to send out at least one signal telling people where we are. Tomorrow, you'll see, we'll have aeroplanes overhead dropping parcels to us.

'Keep your ears open as well as your eyes – if we hear a ship in the darkness we'll send up flares and they'll see them and pick us up.'

And so on.

When such efforts met with neither gratitude nor success, Imeldo tried a different tack. He would carry on baling, he said, until his strength ran out; in the morning the blazing sun they knew so well would complete the drying-out of the raft's floor, and then he would be able to attend properly to his companion's injuries. He would cleanse each wound, he would dress every cut with gauze and bind it with waterproof plasters; there would be no further fear of infection, and soon Epifanio would be good as new. He might as well have been talking to himself. Epifanio's thankless rejoinder was yet another torrent of recrimination. The man's inborn self-obsession was of such depth that he was suffering a quite genuine sense of outrage that his heavenly protectors should have neglected their duty and so nearly allowed him to die. Faced with such egoism, and with the long dark night still ahead of them, Imeldo had a sudden inspiration. He remembered the two lifejackets and, putting one on himself and the other on his companion, he pointed to the whistles attached to the collars.

'Over the open sea the sound of these will carry for miles. We'll take it in turns, and every twenty minutes or so one of us will blow a series of blasts. If we see a light, of course, or hear an engine, we'll blow together so that even in the dark no one can possibly miss us.'

Epifanio responded with surly reluctance, but not even he could contend that blowing a few blasts on a whistle would be too much for him, and so for an hour or two, until optimism ran out, the stillness of the Pacific night was eerily punctuated by a long series of lonely, plaintive curlew calls that might well, had there been anyone there to hear them, have sounded little different from sobs. But nobody was there to hear them, and, before they fell into a fitful sleep, Imeldo, tiring of Epifanio's everlasting litany of self-pity, at last managed to force some measure of pragmatism into their conversation. Slowly, they began to piece together such details as they remembered of the *Berge Istra*'s final voyage, and to speculate as to what might have conspired to bring her to her terrible end.

Chapter Three

IT ALL STARTED AT THE EUROPORT in Rotterdam, where on 13 November 1975 the *Berge Istra* had discharged a cargo of crude oil from Kharg Island in the Persian Gulf, a supply point which later became all too familiar through news bulletins about the recent eight-year war between Iran and Iraq. The plan was that, as usual, the *Istra* should then sail in ballast to Brazil, where she would load up with iron ore at the port of Tubarao before continuing her voyage around the Cape of Good Hope to Kimitsu in Japan. The journey would take about seven weeks, and her estimated date of arrival in Kimitsu was 5 January 1976.

Before she had ever left Rotterdam, however, incidents occurred which indicated that this would be no ordinary voyage. To appreciate their significance, something must be understood of the construction of a supertanker and of the safeguards demanded by commonsense and by maritime law for the protection of both ship and crew from the hazards of carrying volatile and dangerous cargoes. These safeguards include both the installation of scientific safety equipment and standard mandatory procedures relating to its use.

The ship was over 300 yards long, with a maximum width of 166 feet, and everything concerned with the control of her movement and day-to-day management – bridge, engine-room, officers' cabins, galley, crew quarters and recreation rooms – was situated at the stern. Between the bridge and the forepeak lay the 'commercial' section of the vessel, five huge central holds, each with two hatches, port and starboard, which carried both the cargo and the fuel on which the ship herself was run. Flanking these holds on both sides was a string of wing tanks, twenty in all, used only to contain ballast water and oil. As in any other vessel, provision had been made for keeping her on an even keel, and linking the holds were pump-rooms fore and aft to enable the transfer as required of oil or water in the bunkers and bilges. The pipes for such transference ran through a 'double bottom', located beneath the holds. Such, in only layman's detail, was the basic lay-out of the *Berge Istra*.

As in any container of oil, petroleum or similar product, from a supertanker to a cigarette lighter, real danger comes not when it is full but when it is empty of everything but air and the residual vapours from its previous contents. Without the presence of oxygen a can of petrol will neither burn nor explode. A fuel tanker, therefore, is at greatest risk after it has unloaded its cargo, and it is in the procedures for cleaning out the holds and in making certain that such cleaning has been effective that the rules of maritime safety are most stringently laid down.

Again in layman's terms, there are two basic ways of ensuring that a tanker's holds have been rendered free from the risk of explosion after the cargo has been discharged. The first and less satisfactory method, from every point of view but one, is to render the holds 'gas free', a lengthy and unpleasant manual operation, which, by its nature, is open to the risk of human error. First, over a period of several hours, each hold is repeatedly flushed out with jets of steam-heated sea water from a Butterworth system of high-pressure hoses playing at varying heights and distances from the hatches; the waste water is then pumped into the sea. But floating on the surface of this waste will be countless solid lumps of crude oil that cannot be dispersed through the runaway pipes; these are tackled with hand-held shovels and pressed hard against the sides of the hold or tank, later to be removed by hand, loaded into drums, and thrown overboard. The inner surfaces of the holds are finally cleaned and polished by seamen gaining access to them through manholes about two and a half feet in diameter. In the central holds with their flat surfaces this process, though tedious and dirty, presents no great difficulty. But in the curved wing tanks with their confusion of pipes and recesses, spars and cross-members, it is a demanding task that is not always carried out quite as conscientiously as safety would require.

One way and another, therefore, not the easiest or most agreeable of shipboard duties. From the seamen's point of view, however, it does have one attraction. The cleaning-out of the *Berge Istra* after an oil-carrying voyage would have entailed shift-work twenty-four hours a day for a week or more, and that in its turn would have meant extra earnings at overtime rates.

The 'gas free' system is, as its name implies, a method of emptying the holds and tanks of all dangerous substances and residual vapours. More trustworthy and more generally favoured is the 'inert gas' system whereby the holds and tanks, after cleaning, are filled with a non-volatile gas, a depressant, that removes all oxygen and so precludes even the possibility of a subsequent explosion. In order to employ this method of cleaning, however, it is necessary to have a plant for the manufacture of inert gas. The *Berge Istra* had been provided during construction with just such a plant, and had made use of it on her previous voyages, but during the final stages of her last loading at Rotterdam a fault had developed in one of the plant's combustion chambers and repairs had not been carried out by the time the ship set sail.

In addition, another vital item of safety equipment was out of commission and had been put ashore for repair or replacement. The function of this item, known as a servomex unit, was to maintain a constant automatic measurement of the oxygen content and pressure within the holds, and its facilities included both recording systems and alarms. But for this voyage the fully automated system had been replaced by a portable, hand-operated device with an implicit vulnerability to human error – and with no capability of continuously monitoring the oxygen content and pressure below decks.

It was in this condition that, on 14 November 1975, the *Berge Istra* set out for Tubarao in Brazil with her holds carrying only 54,000 tons of ballast and 9,700 tons of fuel oil for the journey.

In the early days of the voyage, however, the dissatisfaction of the lower ranking crewmen, including Imeldo and Epifanio, was centred not upon safety, which after several trouble-free trips they more or less took for granted, but upon money. On previous journeys this had been the stage at which they had earned most of their overtime pay, but now things were different. This time, while they were still cleaning out the central holds, the bosun had appeared with the hand-operated servomex unit. He had taken readings and had then told them that from now on there would be little or no overtime duty. Whereas the practice had always been for men off duty to be employed on the scouring and polishing of the holds, this time it would be left to the men on watch to carry out the job to the best of their ability in the time available.

And so, as Imeldo and Epifanio now remembered, between Rotterdam and Brazil the central holds were not cleaned to their usual standards, and the wing tanks were not cleaned at all. In consequence, overtime earnings amounted to much less than normal, and it was not the happiest of crews that brought the *Berge Istra* to berth in Tubarao at 10.30 hours on the morning of 28 November 1975. But still, they did have their basic wages, and as loading began that same day the men off duty made full use of them in the bars and bordellos of Tubarao's waterfront district, the Barrio de los Cacharros. It was not until the small hours of the next morning that the last of them came back on board, which was hard luck on those who had been over-enthusiastic in their leisure pursuits, for at 5.30 a.m. the bosun, Avelino Torres, a keen and lively twenty-seven-year-old, called the crew together in the smoking-room for an announcement that ended all thoughts of further rest and recreation.

Loading had gone swiftly and well, and the captain had ruled that the voyage would continue without delay. Holds 2, 4, and 5 had already been filled, and the process of closing them down would begin while work was being completed in holds 1 and 3. Crewmen not engaged in either of these routines would start preparations for casting off, and the ship would be made ready to weigh anchor and sail on the afternoon tide. Captain's orders are never a matter for debate, and at 14.50 hours on 29 November 1975 the *Berge Istra* put out to sea from Tubarao with a cargo of 185,244 long tons of iron ore.

That was her commercial cargo, due to be discharged at Kimitsu, Japan, on 5 January 1976. In addition she was carrying 7,500 tons of bunker oil, 390 tons of diesel oil, 200 tons of lubricating oil, and 150 tons of fresh water. The afterpeak contained 300 tons of ballast, and there were 584 tons of waste in the slop tank, Number 10, on the starboard side. She was not, therefore, perfectly in balance, her for'ard draught of 61′ 2″ comparing with an after draught of 59′ 1″, and it was clear that before reaching Kimitsu it would be necessary to transfer oil from fore to aft to trim the vessel on an even keel.

For the first few days, however, with the wind rising and the sea washing over the decks, the duties doled out to the crew seemed more than usually haphazard. Working in groups, no sooner had they settled down to a given task than the bosun would suddenly withdraw one or more of their number to attend to something else. Not a watch went past without some seaman failing to turn up to join shipmates who were expecting and in some cases counting on him, and the general mood was one of mounting irritation. Until, that was, orders came down from Almar Ratama, the Norwegian chief mate: all crew not on essential duties were to be employed on a complete repainting of the ship before she reached Japan. Rumour had it that the owners must be expecting an inspector to come aboard in Kimitsu. But there were no grumbles or complaints, for these new orders meant overtime, and after two weeks of intensive refurbishment the *Berge Istra*, by 20 December 1975, looked, on the surface, as bonnie as a bride.

Below decks, however, down in the holds and engine-room, it was a very different story.

Chapter Four

ON ANY BOAT OR SHIP the constant need to carry out random chores is a simple fact of life, and Imeldo and Epifanio, like their comrades in the crew, were well used to being shifted around as odd-job men on and below deck. What they were not accustomed to was the sort of work that confronted them now.

As far back as January 1975 the *Berge Istra*'s master, Captain Kristoffer Hemnes, had complained to the ship's owners, Sig. Bergesen DY & Co. of Oslo, about severe corrosion in the pipe-work running through the vessel's 'double bottom'. This, he reported, was causing internal leakage of both oil and water. His complaint was acknowledged, but nothing was done. Six months later, in June 1975, Captain Hemnes, this time supported by the Chief Mate Almar Ratama, once again drew the attention of the owners to the corrosion in the pipes, informing them that the deterioration must now be regarded as extremely serious.

It was indeed. When the owners decided against replacing the pipes, which would have put the vessel temporarily out of commission, and opted instead for a makeshift repair job, the damage revealed was remarkable. The holes in the oil lines were such that the initial remedy suggested – patching them with plates – failed to prevent the leakage, and so slightly more sophisticated steps were taken. Rings or collars were fitted around the areas of damage. To reach and, hopefully, to seal these corroded holes, many of the main pipes had to be rotated through ninety degrees, and some through 180. The oil lines were riddled.

Not surprisingly, even this more ambitious example of making do failed and the jobs meted out to the crewmen during the ship's last voyage involved not merely routine care and maintenance but also running repairs including, almost certainly, the welding of splits and fractures in the leaking oil pipes. That the leaks were serious Imeldo and Epifanio remembered only too well, for they had shared the responsibility for wiping them clean. A thankless task, in fact an impossible one, and by 19 December 1975 Captain Hemnes was once again protesting to the owners. In a radio message sent that day he reported severe damage in the Number 9 port and starboard tanks and requested that replacement pipes be awaiting installation at Kimitsu, their port of arrival.

How much rubbish was by now slopping around in the 'double bottom' may only be guessed at, but a statement made by the *Berge Istra*'s former chief engineer, a Norwegian named Hospeth who had left the ship in Rotterdam reveals that, 'when she sailed from Rotterdam in November 1975, as a result of the damaged piping about twenty tons of waste oil and water had accumulated in the "double bottom"'. Damage apart, the last recorded cleaning out of the ship's slop tank had been in April/May 1974, more than eighteen months before her final, fatal journey, and in that tank, Number 10 on the starboard side, was a further 500 tons and more of old waste material.

Nor was it only the pipe-work that was giving cause for concern. Faults were developing in the engine-room, and for two long and expensive days the *Berge Istra* lay idle in the water while repairs were carried out to damaged connecting-rods, a failing familiar on a lesser scale to almost everyone who has ever owned a second-hand motor car. Any travelling salesman who has suffered such a misfortune will readily understand the eagerness of the *Berge Istra*'s master to be on his way again as quickly as possible, effecting all repairs, other than those needed to get the vessel moving, while she was once again in transit, so making up for lost time. For time, in the shipping trade as in any other, is money.

One incident firmly embedded in the survivors' memories came three days later on 22 December 1975, for that was when the leakage very nearly changed from a problem to a crisis. Working with other seamen on routine deck duties, they received a brusque order from the bosun:

'Drop everything and get below – there's a bad leakage in the lines.'

A new crack had opened in one of the supply lines, and the ship's drinking water was being polluted with oil. In the blazing heat of the Pacific, many days' sailing from their port of destination, this could of course spell disaster. Imeldo, Epifanio and the others were told to check every inch of the lines for further spillage, but even more urgently, the existing crack had to be sealed before the pollution could spread throughout the entire fresh water supply of the ship. And that was why neither Imeldo nor Epifanio could ever be in the slightest doubt that welding had been permitted both on and below decks, even though the *Berge Istra* was sailing without benefit of the 'inert gas' system of safety. They had stood beside the welder at work with his torch in the 'double bottom', and at the time they, like everyone else aboard, had been profoundly thankful to him.

Now, however, alone on their raft, they began to speculate, to link cause with effect, and to wonder if there might be some connection between such risky practices and the explosions; they had, after all, seen the welder busy on the hatches only minutes before the *Berge Istra* had been blown apart.

But daylight was breaking, and they had to face up to the grim reality of their first full day as survivors of a shipwreck, alone in the middle of the Molucca Sea, many hundreds of miles from anywhere.

Chapter Five

THE DAY TO WHICH THEY WOKE was 31 December 1975, the last of the old year, but even a Scot would have had difficulty raising his spirits to greet the new one facing Imeldo and Epifanio. But Imeldo did his best.

'Have a biscuit,' he said brightly as dawn broke, and opened the first of their five edible packets.

'And a drink,' he added, broaching the second of the sixteen precious half-litre cans.

Epifanio stared at him in blank bewilderment. 'That's all?'

'That's all if we want to get out of this. God only knows how long these rations may have to last. One biscuit a day should do us, two at the very most, and the water comes in sips, not gulps.'

Epifanio's grudging acceptance stemmed less from acquiescence than from dumbfounded astonishment. By noon, however, his mood of reason had evaporated in the sun, and he was angrily demanding another 'meal'.

'But Epifanio, you can count. At the rate you're after, these biscuits won't last four days.'

'So what? You said yourself there'll be ships and aeroplanes already looking for us, and we'll be picked up long before the food runs out. Look, that damn biscuit just melted away in my mouth – I need one in the morning, one right now, and another at night. Christ, man, I'm starving. The good Lord won't forsake us, our saints won't let us die, so give me another one now.'

If a crippled man lying on his back in a puddle of filth could swagger, Epifanio Perdomo López would have been swaggering now, his commonsense in abeyance and his arrogance and self-esteem bolstered by the conviction that he was someone special and that it was no more than Heaven's bounden duty to see him safely through.

Imeldo brought him rudely back to reality. 'If you eat three, then I'll eat three, that way we'll soon be starving together. Or if you prefer, we'll drink all the water we want to, and that way we'll die of thirst. For God's sake, man, use your head. There's no telling how long we may be out here before they find us – let's at least try to make sure we're still alive when they do.'

The argument developed swiftly into an angry quarrel, which fostered a deep and growing hostility that was to poison the relationship between the two men throughout all but the last hours of their ordeal. Epifanio relapsed into a sullen silence, punctured by occasional broody mutterings, and by late afternoon Imeldo was glad to seize upon an unexpected change in the weather as a chance to ease the mounting tension with a joke. Since daybreak the sea had been calm, but for more than an hour now dark clouds had been gathering windward, and with the approach of dusk a fitful breeze brought them gradually overhead. Before long the water was tossing and chopping, and without further warning they were in the throes of a tropical storm. The raft was heaving and pitching, the seas pouring in over the shallow sides, and within seconds both men were drenched and dispirited, crouching terrified in a swirling tub of oil and water. It was then that Imeldo again proved himself to be a man with both guts and backbone.

'It looks,' he shouted over the raging wind, 'as if we're going to celebrate New Year's Eve with a dance.'

There was no response from his companion, who was still wrapped in silence, smouldering with resentment.

Just before nightfall Imeldo tried yet again to bring some reason to their relationship and to Epifanio's behaviour. His unskilled efforts at first aid had proved less than effective in protecting Epifanio's injuries from the oily muck rolling back and forth across the floor of the raft, particularly the deep gashes on his legs. The growing danger of infection was obvious, and so despite the unruly bucketing of the raft Imeldo turned once again to the survival pack.

'Hold still just a minute, Epifanio. There's no way we can keep these wounds of yours clean, so I'm going to give you an injection to stop them turning septic.'

His patient reacted like a madman. 'Keep away from me, you're not sticking any needles in me. Leave me alone, or stick it in yourself. What I want is food, and I want it right now.'

Epifanio was beside himself, but his injuries, luckily, held him physically in check. Replacing the ampoule in the emergency pack, Imeldo simply ignored him, and Epifanio retreated once again into truculent silence.

With nightfall the storm gathered force and the rain changed from a steady downpour to a deafening, thundering barrage. It beat down on them like blows, flattening them, pinning them helplessly to the floor of the raft, where all they could do was hang on, pray and try to breathe. Any thought of bailing out was impossible. Water came at them from above and from every side as their little platform rocked, leaping and bucketing in the tossing waves. Imeldo's brave New Year's dance had become a frenzied rigadoon.

Hour after hour it went on until at last, tormented almost beyond endurance by thoughts of his wife and children who were no doubt singing in the New Year and wishing and praying for his safe return, Imeldo sought distraction by attempting the task of bailing out. But it was a hopeless effort as for every scoopful of water he succeeded in throwing over the side another ton came pouring in. Finally, in sheer desperation and loneliness, he made one further move towards his surly co-sufferer.

'Epifanio,' he said, putting an arm round the man's shoulders and hoisting him carefully to a sitting position, his back propped against the shallow wall, 'this is New Year's Eve, and out of all the ship's company we're the only ones alive to see it. Let's think for a few minutes of our friends and be thankful for our luck. We're still here, Epifanio – come on, let's welcome the New Year with a toast to the future.'

Without waiting for a response he pushed forward a biscuit – tentatively, like a child feeding buns to an elephant – and supported his shipmate's lolling head as he helped him to sip a few precious mouthfuls of water. It was a brave effort, which, for once, met with due reward. Epifanio wolfed the biscuit, savoured the fresh water like champagne, and muttered a few rough words of gratitude as he leaned back against Imeldo's encircling arm. The two men clung together, weeping, and then Imeldo steadied his emotions and proposed the formal toast.

'A Happy New Year to you, brother.'

'A Happy New Year, and may God hear you, Imeldo.'

These were almost the last words of goodwill Imeldo was to hear for weeks ahead, and he may have suspected as much as he crouched in the pouring rain. Wistfully his mind turned back to the last great festival, Christmas, only one short week behind them and yet a whole world and lifetime away.

Chapter Six

WITH THE PROBLEMS OF 22 December contained if not cured, Captain Hemnes and the crew of the *Berge Istra* began to look forward to the festival ahead and the traditional party that would be held on Christmas Eve.

There were twenty-nine men and three women on board, a small-sounding complement for such an enormous vessel as the *Istra*, yet all that was needed in this age of computers and high technology. The captain and all the officers but one were Norwegian; the exception, the radio officer, was the only Briton. Michael LeMarche, born thirty-four years earlier in the Channel Islands, was perhaps the most popular character on the ship, well thought of by officers and men alike, respected for his professional expertise and admired for the cool courage with which, on a different vessel, he had climbed the mainmast in a storm to release a trapped radar aerial, a dangerous task that might very easily have been delegated to a lesser member of the crew. Both he and his young wife Sandra felt a close affinity with the Norwegian people and whenever the *Berge Istra* made her home port in Scandinavia, Michael LeMarche would find Sandra, with a rented caravan, waiting there to greet his arrival. Of the men in the crew, twelve, including the bosun, were Spanish; there was one Brazilian seaman and the repairman/welder, Rene Govaerts, was Belgian. His fiancée Paula Janssen, who was also Belgian, was one of the three women aboard, all of whom were stewardesses. The others were Pia-Elena Lofquist of Sweden and

Carmen Sevrlica from Yugoslavia, who was married to one of her own countrymen Egidij Sevrlica, the ship's electrician.

In high spirits the crew, and the three girls in particular, threw themselves into the welcome distraction of preparing for the Christmas party. The lounges and mess rooms were hoovered, dusted and polished; streamers, stars and tinsel were hung from the ceilings and walls. In the galley the cook and his voluntary helpers brought muscle and imagination to the preparation of virtually the one meal that would be shared by officers and men together in an all-ranks jollification that would last the night. For Michael LeMarche, too, it was the busy season, as man after man queued up to enlist his aid in sending festive greetings to their wives and families at home.

If Captain Hemnes at this time was a worried man – and there is irrefutable evidence that he was – he was also an exemplary commanding officer, and no hint of his anxiety was allowed to spoil the enjoyment of his crew. This considerate self-discipline, was, as Imeldo remembered, typical of Kristoffer Hemnes, 'A tall, white-haired, good-humoured man, the ideal captain. Passing through narrow straits he was never nervous; smoking his pipe, sharing a joke or a greeting, he would stroll around the ship passing on his confidence and friendly calm to the crew.'

By 24 December, however, Captain Hemnes had already, for reasons that are still unexplained, dispensed with an important maritime practice and precaution to which he had been an enthusiastic subscriber on previous voyages. It was not known to such as Imeldo and Epifanio, and would have meant nothing to them if it had been. The atmosphere aboard the *Berge Istra* was festive, and the Christmas party went with a swing. After a fine and formal dinner all ranks off duty congregated in the bar to let their hair down, and the three girls, well-suited to life with a shipload of sailors, really came into their own, displaying a good humoured understanding of the difference in temperament between the proud, passionate, volatile Spaniards, Europe's greatest natural exponents of the art and feeling of the fiesta, and their superior officers the Norwegians, who were more reserved, slower to thaw – but no strangers themselves to long nights when the welkin rings.

Perhaps stirred by the operatic connotations of her name, the electrician's effervescent Yugoslavian wife Carmen made a point of dancing with each Spanish crewman before offering the same privilege to his officers. The repairman/welder's Belgian fiancée Paula, who was some years older, made tactful use of her greater experience to cajole out of his shyness or exaggerated respect any masculine wallflower who seemed to be holding back. Pia-Elena, the bright and bubbly twenty-three-year-old from Sweden, simply enjoyed herself, at the same time doing her considerable best to ensure that everyone else did the same. The *Berge Istra* that evening was a happy ship, and the dancing went on until daybreak.

It takes more than the dawn, however, to silence a Spaniard in the full flow of a fiesta, and when the floor was cleared and the bar was closed the men from Tenerife then gathered in a corner of the lounge to continue the wassail with flamenco. Ramon Herrera Fernandez, the forty-one-year-old motorman, regaled his homesick compatriots with songs and ballads of the Canary Islands sung in his resonant baritone, for which he provided his own guitar accompaniment. His recital was interrupted only by the explosive arrival of a grotesque, prancing, primping creature in fancy dress.

'Remember, Epifanio,' urged Imeldo, 'how at first we just couldn't imagine who it could be? That enormous blonde wig, those strings of beads, the lavish make-up, the floral skirts reaching down to the ankles? We should have guessed, of course – who else would it be but Mister LeMarche?' And

Michael LeMarche indeed it had been, the sort of high-spirited young officer no ship can ever afford to be without.

But here on the raft Epifanio was thinking of something else, something more significant than even the best of celebrations. Parties must come to an end, and on 26 December he was once again standing watch on the bridge, a duty that had started at 4.00 p.m. and would continue until he was relieved by José Ferrer at 8.00 p.m. Until now this had always been a simple matter of routine involving little more than being present with his eyes open, but since 22 December a completely new procedure had been added to his duties.

In future, the chief mate had ordered, at 7.00 p.m. each evening Epifanio was to open the covers on hatches 6, 7, and 8 on the port side, and twelve hours later, when he reported back for morning watch, he was to close them again.

Puzzled at first by this seemingly pointless instruction, Epifanio, on carrying it out, soon fathomed its purpose. As he opened each hatch lid, a device rather like a lavatory cover, he was greeted by a loud 'popping' noise and the strong, sour smell of gas – so pungent it forced him to turn his head sideways to escape it – and it was clear that pressure was building up dangerously on the port side of the ship. On the following night the story was the same: despite the earlier twelve hours of ventilation, the opening of the hatch covers released loud 'popping' and a rancid smell – the fumes in the hold were still rising under pressure.

For once, the brooding, angry silence of Epifanio was not without justification.

Chapter Seven

'Do you remember, Imeldo,' mused Epifanio, 'what was happening on deck just before everything went crazy?'

'Can't say I do – not exactly.'

'Well, I do. As we walked to work the welder was fitting a drip-tray round the port hatches. In fact he'd been at it for several days and the holds he was working over were the ones I'd been opening and shutting every night and morning, the ones the gas was escaping from.'

It was then that Imeldo did begin to remember, to recall the small but important safeguard that seemed to have been omitted from the *Berge Istra*'s design specifications, and certainly from her original construction. The intake or delivery of oil can be a messy business, and during her early voyages one unnecessary hazard had soon become obvious to all; oil pipes are not easy things to handle, the flow can not be cut off completely in an instant, so spillage is inevitable when the lines are disconnected from the stand-pipes. Allowed to run overboard this leakage will pollute the water of the harbour, perhaps even, if not checked quickly, of the surrounding coastline. If the spillage is inboard, the deck around the delivery pipes can be swiftly transformed into a slippery skid-pan, with obvious danger to the men working around the holds.

This problem had been noted by the master and owners, and during the *Istra*'s penultimate voyage steps had been taken to alleviate it – but only on the starboard side. There a series of curving metal plates with rims eight inches high had been joined together in a U-pattern to form trays 3' 6" wide around the intake and delivery pipes. Oil leaking into these trays would be collected in buckets and poured into the storage tank. The trays had been welded to the deck while the ship was at sea.

On the final voyage, as the two survivors now remembered, the same process had been started on the port side of the vessel, only days before and continuing right up to the moment of disaster. Only half an hour before the first explosion Epifanio, on his way to the foredeck, had noticed that the welder was using an electrode rod to seal loose plates to the deck around Number 8 hold, and he had noticed, too, that the work was within about four feet of completion.

'About time, too,' had been his characteristic reaction. 'Every other ship I've ever sailed on has had trays like these already fitted. And they have the gall to call this bucket "fully automated".'

Epifanio was a healthier man mentally when his truculence was thus directed and his grousing was not without reason – but now, on the raft, after only some forty hours adrift, his paranoia, without sense or logic, was already creeping ominously towards the point of real danger. The first signs, inevitably, related to his physical condition, and his running battle against Imeldo's discipline gathered both force and virulence as the first day of January wore wearily on.

'I can't bear this any longer, Imeldo. My legs hurt terribly.'

'No wonder, since you won't use your head and let me help you. Good God, man, your legs hurt me, too, because they're starting to smell. Can't you see the pus seeping out of them?

Here, right here, I have injections that might clear them up – won't you at least give it a try?'

He could have chosen no more disastrous line of appeal, and the sensor-needle of Epifanio's emotional imbalance flickered up to near-hysteria.

'Those injections are poison – they're meant to do away with men who're dying and can't stand the agony any longer. That's what you really want, isn't it? You want me to die so's you can have my share of the water and biscuits.'

'Don't be such a bloody fool, Epifanio.' Imeldo's rising anger, coupled with his companion's immobility, was giving him new-found courage and authority. 'We'll live together, or we'll die together – can't you see that? And if we don't start helping each other, I know damned well which one it's likely to be.

'Look, if you're determined not to have an injection, if you'd rather risk losing your legs, I'm not going to try and force you. But at least shut up, lie still, and let me wash these cuts out – it makes me sick just to look at them, they're not just sore, they're disgusting.'

Without waiting for an answer Imeldo dipped an empty water can over the side, filled it with brine, and in grim silence began to wipe the oil and yellow-green pus from Epifanio's suppurating lacerations.

Jolted out of his arrogance, Epifanio switched targets. Almost every Spaniard has his chosen saints, associated variously with his name, his date of birth or his place of origin. Epifanio's favourites were the Virgin of Candelaria, patron of the Canaries, whose shrine is in Tenerife, and Our Lady of the Snows, whose sanctuary is on the neighbouring island of La Palma but who is also represented by an image in the village where he had been born. Both sanctified figures, having failed so far to meet their obligations, were now subjected to censure interspersed with occasional renewed appeals made, presumably, as a sort of spiritual hedging bet.

Imeldo preferred to pin his hopes on secular assistance. 'There must be dozens of Japanese fishing boats working in this area. You'll see, we'll be picked up tomorrow, or the next day at the latest. But for now, use a bit of sense. Your legs are infected, Epifanio – if you're so scared of the needle, at least take one of these pills.

Epifanio's reaction was as before. 'Leave me alone, I tell you. Don't come near me, just leave me in peace and let me die alone when God calls me, and not before.'

It was tedious, and it was trying, and as nightfall approached it grew steadily worse. Epifanio's mouthings became an endless, self-pitying whine.

'Imeldo, why did you drag me from the sea? Why did you bathe me and bandage me when you could see I was hurt beyond endurance? In the water I was no longer suffering. I was already dead. Why did you bring me back to life?'

Why indeed? Imeldo would have been less than human not to have asked himself the same question. Yet still he controlled his anger and began to outline the procedure they must follow throughout the hours of darkness, repeating that they were drifting in latitudes frequented by the Japanese fishing fleet.

'We must keep watch all the time. Just think what a tragedy it would be if a ship passed close by without seeing us, just because we were asleep and had sent no signal. How would we feel if we suddenly woke to see help disappearing into the distance? Look, I don't expect you to share the job equally – you go off to sleep, I'll take first turn and make it last as long as I can hold out. You'll probably only have to stand the last hour or so before daybreak.'

'To hell with the last hour, and to hell with keeping watch. How can you expect me to do that? My head is aching, my legs are useless, my belly is empty and I can't even sit up straight. Forget about tonight – I just want it to be tomorrow.' Epifanio was contemptuous of his companion's insistence on self-help.

Imeldo stared at him. 'Christ, man, the sun's only been down for an hour. You expect it to rise early, especially for you?'

Sarcasm was wasted as whilst they had been arguing the seas had slowly been rising higher and higher. The waves were now towering twenty feet above them and the raft was being tossed as if on a giant switchback. Quite suddenly a new dimension was added to Epifanio's moral disintegration and to Imeldo's deep-rooted fear. The injured man's voice rose to a banshee-like shriek and as Imeldo watched horrified he curled himself up like a snake, closing his eyes, burying his head in his arms, shutting out everything around him, and let out a wail beyond all human comprehension. But one thing Imeldo did comprehend, all too clearly, was that his initial fear of Epifanio had not been ill-founded. Sometime, eventually, he himself must sleep, yet Epifanio lay only inches away from him, sobbing and screaming so much it was clear that he was no longer in control of himself. Imeldo steeled himself to stay awake, praying that the night would pass quickly, that the storm would abate, and that his dreadful shipmate would scream himself into exhaustion.

None of his prayers were to be answered. Crying out now that the water pouring over him was freezing, Epifanio roughly snatched the plastic sheeting, their sole protection, and wrapped himself in it like a mummy, only to call out moments later that the covering itself was icy cold and that this, surely, was Death approaching. Looking at him lying there stark-eyed as if in his coffin, Imeldo for a moment almost began to believe him, but then Epifanio came suddenly and briefly to his senses and began to help. Between them they raised the sheeting and draped it like a tent over the four metal struts sticking up from the floor, huddling together beneath it. But for guy ropes and pegs this tent had only their exhausted arms and half-frozen fingers, and time after time the plastic was torn from their grasp by the wind. It wreathed itself around them like a shroud, it tangled itself in their arms and legs, and it threw them helplessly around in the heaving, foul slough on the floor of the raft.

Yet it may be that perhaps Imeldo's prayers were, after all, being answered. In the immediate fight for survival, and while the danger was at its height Imeldo, scarcely believing it, began to realize that Epifanio, wounds and suspicions forgotten, was battling with the elements just as bravely as he was himself. As dawn broke on 2 January 1976, these two peasants from the Canaries, natural enemies in outlook and beliefs but Spanish to the core, found themselves sharing the all-too-rare experience of fighting shoulder to shoulder, each for the other, instead of hand to hand.

Of course it couldn't last. By mid-morning the weather had worsened still further. Epifanio had reverted to type, and a new, eerie danger had presented itself.

At first it was merely physical. The storm had gone insane, and the problem was no longer how to withstand the buffeting from one side of the raft to the other, but how to stay within it at all. Light and fragile, it was being batted like a shuttlecock from one wave's crest to the next. Epifanio, lying flat, was the safer of its two occupants, but if Imeldo, half-upright of necessity and the likelier candidate for summary ejection, had been thrown overboard, then Epifanio's life expectancy, too, could have been reckoned in seconds. It was a situation calling for urgent action and Imeldo, the timid, indecisive Imeldo, somehow summoned up the courage to initiate it.

Afraid, and with good reason, that his motives might be misunderstood, he nevertheless hauled in a length of rope trailing over the side and, laying his bodyweight over Epifanio, began binding his companion to two of the struts sticking up from the floor. Although he protested furiously, Epifanio had no strength for real resistance, and finally let himself be tethered, yielding like a sulky, mistrustful child. Epifanio's eyes, nonetheless, were glaring, and so as he bound himself to a strut in the far corner of the raft Imeldo made quite certain that he had allowed himself some freedom of movement and that his arms would be unhampered in whatever emergency might come next.

Chapter Eight

HE DID NOT HAVE LONG to wait for it. As midday approached Epifanio resumed his ritual reproach about the rations, making a few days of hunger sound like the tortures of the damned. He could not last out, he protested, on such a meagre diet. Imeldo tried first to placate him with a reminder that 'lunchtime' was close, but when this met only with another torrent of abuse he decided it was time for Epifanio to face reality.

'I have news for you, my friend. We have, in fact, been far too generous to ourselves, and things are beginning to look bad. We've been out here less than three days, and already we've used up half the food and water. We've seen neither ship nor aircraft, and we might as well get used to the idea that it's going to be a long wait. From now on we share one biscuit for each meal. If you get hungry that's just too bad – it's our only chance.'

The subsequent argument raged for a full half-hour, by which time the sun was directly overhead. Taking a packet of biscuits from the emergency locker, Imeldo withdrew just one and concentrated intensely, despite the rocking of the raft, on dividing it meticulously into two equal parts. His concentration almost cost them dear. Epifanio, beside himself with hunger, fury and frustration, lunged forward on his restraining ropes and managed somehow to grasp hold of the packet. For what seemed an eternity the two men struggled to wrest the packet from the other, while the prize they were fighting over threatened to crumble into sodden, inedible mush as a sudden rainfall poured down on them. Finally Imeldo, because of his greater range of movement, succeeded in wrenching the mangled package from his opponent – but two minutes later, as he slumped winded in the furthest corner of the raft, he began almost to wish that he had failed.

The figure crouching opposite him, straining against the ropes, looked less like a man than a trapped and cornered animal. The staring eyes were red-rimmed and glittering with hatred. Then Epifanio, in a crazed, high-pitched, choking voice uttered the words Imeldo had been dreading since the moment he had first recognized his companion in misfortune.

'You know I can't live on half a biscuit, but you don't care – because that's the way you want it. But now I know something, too, Imeldo – I know what I have to do.'

Like a rabbit facing a stoat, Imeldo stared into Epifanio's eyes and remembered the stories he had heard about him. He recalled the reason a former member of the *Istra*'s crew, Manuel Linares, had given him for quitting the ship at Las Palmas. 'I'm leaving, Imeldo, because I won't sail any further with that man Epifanio. He terrifies me. He's already killed one man, and he's proud of the time that had earned him in prison. You watch out for him, Imeldo, and don't ever quarrel with him because he's dangerous.'

Summoning up courage he never dreamed he possessed, Imeldo resolutely ironed out the tremors in his voice. 'What do you have in mind Epifanio? To steal all the biscuits when I'm asleep – or do you mean to kill me?'

His companion's response was a muttered repetition of his earlier threat. 'You'll find out soon enough. I know what I have to do. I know what I have to do.'

Warily watching, Imeldo slowly, reluctantly, began to weigh up options that, only days before, would never have entered his mind. He didn't want to bully or oppress his injured shipmate, already hurt badly enough. He wanted still less – *dear God, what sort of thinking was this?* – to dispose of him. But, there could be no denying it, he was now desperately afraid for his own safety, and it was hard not to see in Epifanio a danger even greater than the storm still howling around them.

As if reading his mind Epifanio suddenly spoke again. 'I know what I have to do. I know what I have to do,' he croaked.

There was a horrible, menacing intensity in the voice and in the man's unwavering stare. Imeldo gazed feverishly all around him as if searching for some avenue of escape. It was at that moment, purely by chance, that his eyes focused on the survival pack on his lap. Suddenly he knew, with a sense of awful inevitability, exactly what he, not Epifanio, had to do.

Lying there in front of him were two pieces of survival equipment – a small pair of surgical scissors and a clasp-knife six inches long. In that instant they were transformed in his mind from potential life-savers into deadly weapons. He forced himself, for a few clear seconds, to think rationally, to assess the true extent of the danger, and always the answer came up the same. Sometime, perhaps very soon, he was bound to fall asleep leaving Epifanio awake and dangerous. Not only that, the storm, eventually, must die down. He could not keep Epifanio tethered for days and nights like a wild animal, for allowed no movement his limbs would wither, his blood would stop flowing, and he would surely die. Yet Epifanio had made his murderous intentions all too clear. No, there was no choice; what had to be done must be done, regardless of the consequences.

The scissors were really very small. Huddling forward over the survival pack as if to shield it from the water still rushing in over the raft, Imeldo surreptitiously withdrew them from the plastic drum and secreted them securely beneath the belt and waistband of his trousers. There, pressed tight against his belly, they would be safe from thieving hands even while he lay asleep.

But the knife, now that was a different story. Sturdy, strong-bladed and lethal, it was a positive incitement to violence, perhaps even – why not? – to murder. Looking at it lying there bulky in his lap, he knew it could never be hidden away effectively in his skimpy, tattered clothing. Imeldo made up his mind, drew a deep breath, and with a great shout midway between madness and exultation he seized the knife by its haft and flung it far into the sea.

Then, wondering if perhaps he and not Epifanio had gone mad, he sat back bewildered, scarcely believing what he had done, until, drawing slowly over him like a warm blanket, there came the comforting realization that now he could, at last, go safely to sleep.

Chapter Nine

IT WAS LONG INTO THE NEXT DAY BEFORE another word passed between them, and Imeldo began to find Epifanio's stubborn, smouldering silence scarcely less tolerable than the ranting and raving that had gone before. The man was once again wrapped in the plastic sheeting, so at least there was no danger of a sudden attack, but what thoughts, what plans, for God's sake, were being mulled over in his mind? With a sudden guilty start Imeldo realized that this was precisely what he himself was doing – weighing up the dangers of being left alone against the fact that the remaining food, used sparingly, could enable one man, but not two, to last out for probably another ten days? Was Epifanio counting on his built-in aggression, and the greater strength of his arms, to see him through if it came to a close combat fight to the death? This was sheer madness, the stuff of bad movies – but lunacy or not, it was a very real possibility.

Without warning Epifanio began to writhe in his ropes, struggling to hoist himself upright. Imeldo braced himself to face whatever attack was coming. Then, freeing his chest and arms, Epifanio leaned forward, twisting his lips in an effort to speak. 'Imeldo,' he croaked, 'I desperately need to shit.'

Imeldo roared with sudden laughter and relief. From the saints to the shithouse, strange bridges span the gulf between antagonists. 'And so you shall, so you shall. But let's think how we go about it.'

'I haven't got time to think about it. I've been holding this in for hours in bloody agony, and I'm either going to mess myself or burst. Please, Imeldo, please give me a hand.'

'Hang on just a few more seconds.' Imeldo was thinking fast. Epifanio's leg wounds were raw and gaping, and fouling himself would be not only degrading but dangerous. *Thank God he had hung on to the scissors.*

Fumbling in his waistband he located them and reached forward and cut a square of plastic from the sheeting. He then cautiously loosened the ropes around Epifanio's waist binding him to the struts. He knelt directly in front of the moaning figure and thrust the fragment of plastic into his hand. 'Here – drag down your pants and shove this under your arse. Now – put both hands on my shoulders, haul yourself up an inch or two, and get on with it.'

It was all over in a few explosive, smelly seconds, and as the tattered makeshift bedpan went sailing over the side Epifanio, for once, seemed to realize just how much was being done for him. 'Thanks, my friend, thanks a thousand times for that. If you only knew how long I held on to myself, thinking I'd bust my guts before even speaking to you, let alone asking for help. I really mean it, Imeldo – thanks a lot.'

'That's all right.' Imeldo's voice was gruff. 'No need for thanks – just remember next time you feel bloody-minded, and try to realize I'm doing the best I can for both of us, not just for myself.'

It was like talking to a child, and the whine was soon back in Epifanio's voice. 'I'll try, Imeldo, honestly I will, but I get so hungry. Why, right now I could eat two kilos of steak and drink five litres of water.'

Imeldo grunted, wanting no more talk about food. It never seemed to occur to Epifanio that he, too, was hungry and would have liked more than a broken biscuit. 'If you did, you'd either choke yourself or die of indigestion.'

'Better that than starvation. At least I'd die content.'

'Christ, you can't even live content.'

Hour after hour the storm continued with the rain pouring down on them. They made a brief attempt to catch some of it in the plastic sheeting, but soon gave it up as useless. With both men falling about and the waves washing over the raft, the best they could hope to husband was a tiny, filthy mixture of fresh water, brine, oil and grease, and there was also the constant risk that the sheeting would be plucked from their grasp and blown away. Exhausted, they lay under a sky so dark that they scarcely noticed the slow transition into another night.

Epifanio, in fact, did not notice it at all, for after their failure to catch even a cupful of drinkable water he had retreated into his plastic lair, his head buried in its folds and with only his incessant moaning to show that he was still alive. Imeldo sat alone, straining his inflamed, salt-rimmed eyes and praying that the long flashes of lightning that tore the black fabric of the night would reveal the outline of a ship. He saw nothing but the curling, towering waves and the human bundle huddled only inches away from him on the heaving, pitching, half-submerged floor of the raft.

Dawn, however, on 4 January brought a quick stab of hope. Shaking Epifanio by the shoulder Imeldo shouted excitedly, 'Get out from under that sheet. Just look at this – we have company.'

Circling over them, swooping closer and closer until they were almost within touching distance, was a flight of birds. Imeldo's heart was leaping. 'Don't you see, we must be close to land. Perhaps even right in amongst the islands.'

He should have known better. Both his ornithology and

practical psychology were at fault. The birds, which he did not recognize, were almost certainly migratory and very possibly hundreds of miles from shore. Epifanio's reaction, too, was what by now he should have learned to expect. Instead of hope he saw only bitter contrast, and in a great wail of self-pity he cried out over and over again, 'Oh, you lucky, lucky birds – how I wish I had wings like you.' He then burst into sobs, buried his face in his hands, and disappeared yet again into his private darkness beneath the plastic covers.

What new terrors obsessed him as he hid there hour after hour, refusing even the pretence of sharing the watch, became immediately clear when Imeldo at last aroused him for the first shared biscuit of the day. Bluster and fury had momentarily given way to a show of resignation and gentle reproach, the usual screams of outrage replaced this time by the wheedling of the humble supplicant.

'Since you're still determined to go on hoarding the biscuits, I'll most surely be the first to die. My legs – just look at them – are rotting away, and I'm weak from loss of blood. Let me ask you just one thing – when I go, don't throw me over the side. Keep my body with you in the raft so that, if a ship does come, it can carry me back to my family in Taganana.'

'Keep you in the raft?'

'No, wait, Imeldo, wait. If I start to smell after a few days, just wrap me in the plastic sheet with a rope around my waist and pull me along behind. That way I can keep you company at least until the sharks take me.'

'Thanks, Epifanio. That would be a great comfort to me. You'd be fine company.'

Gritting his teeth, determined to control himself, Imeldo rummaged in the survival pack, found the primitive fishing tackle, and began threading a line through the eyes of the hooks in preparation against the day when the sea must, finally, die down. Such painstaking endeavour might never yield any profit – but at least it would help him to keep his hands from Epifanio's throat.

Chapter Ten

RESTRAINT SOON PROVED, LIKE VIRTUE, to be its own reward, and early in the morning of 5 January Imeldo found good, if terrifying, reason to be thankful that he still had a companion, however disagreeable.

The sea, at least for the moment, had lost the worst of its wildness, and he became slowly aware that the raft was floating lopsided and swinging around apparently of its own volition. At first he put this down to the more or less static weight of Epifanio, for ever lying prostrate in the same position, but then he realized that the general tendency of movement was in the opposite direction, and closer investigation seemed called for.

Inboard, although the raft was a shambles, nothing appeared worse than it had been before, so Imeldo, holding fast to a strut, leaned cautiously over the side. For several moments he stared in disbelief and then, with a moan of despair, slumped back in near collapse. The raft was breaking up. Down one side of its cellular fabric was a wide, gaping rent. It had doubtless been there, though much smaller, since the very beginning. He had seen, even as he crawled aboard it, that the raft had been badly battered when flung from the ship. But it had amounted to nothing like this. Even in the flat seas of that first afternoon, even in his state of shock, he could not possibly have failed to notice such damage as now confronted him. The little platform, moreover, had supported him on an even keel.

Now it was swinging from side to side like a drunk and, worse still, it was sagging in the middle. Again he leaned cautiously over the side, and again he groaned at what he saw. The savage buffeting of the past few days had taken its toll, and from the apex of the huge main fracture another split, as yet little more than a crack, ran downwards and along, diminishing beneath the bottom of the raft. Relentlessly twisted and tossed by the mountainous seas, their refuge was tearing itself in two.

'Epifanio – wake up, and listen to me.'

A scowling face poked out reluctantly from under the covers. 'What now, for God's sake?'

'We're in trouble, real trouble, and this time you've just got to help me if you want to remain alive.'

'It's that serious?'

'It's not just serious, it's critical, and I mean it. If you want to live more than an hour or two, forget about your legs, yell to your saints, and do exactly what I tell you.'

Imeldo untied Epifanio's bonds and fastened him loosely, instead, to a single strut; he freed his own safety-rope and held it in his hands. He directed one last searching look at his partner, wondering how far he could trust him and yet knowing he had no choice, and taking a deep breath thrust his upper body over the rim of the raft while Epifanio gripped him firmly – he hoped – by the ankles.

Beneath the heaving surface of the water, Imeldo saw at once what he had to do – but how to do it and whether he could do it were different matters indeed. With a struggle that taxed his weakening muscles he hauled himself back inboard, managed some sort of encouraging grin, and murmured, half to himself, 'Now, by God, for both of us, it really is shit or bust.'

He picked up another length of rope, thanking God that

there were several, and trailed it over the opposite side of the raft. Then, with another deep breath and with a further, final appeal to Epifanio, he launched himself into the first of a long, agonizing series of duck-dives, his head, his shoulders, and most of his body dipping and wriggling further and further over the side and under the floor of the raft. Time after time he thought his lungs would burst, whilst effort after effort failed as he fumbled with numb fingers. Always he was terrifyingly aware that if Epifanio should, for one second, loosen his grip, he would drown – in this still-turbulent sea there was no possible hope of recovery. Yet still Imeldo battled on and on until the two trailing ropes were at last knotted and the torn and breaking structure of the raft held together.

Even in his moment of triumph, however, he knew in his heart that it was not enough, that the destructive power of the waves would not be held in check by a length of line. As he lay back exhausted, he wondered in despair whether this dangerous operation had in fact been worth all the fear and effort.

This was a bad time for Imeldo, a time when all his courage and resolution threatened to collapse under the sheer weight of despair. He had faced danger, conquered fear, performed tasks no man should be asked to perform – and for what? Probably, at best, a few more hours of dire discomfort and increasing terror whilst they waited for the moment when the raft would finally rip itself in two and he and Epifanio, each clinging to his useless fragment, would watch one another spinning away to inevitable death.

Everything seemed so unfair. Surely after such efforts he might have expected a little help from Heaven; had Epifanio perhaps been right after all in feeling that the saints were not really pulling their weight? He checked himself angrily; this smacked of blasphemy. And in that moment he felt a sudden wild surge of hope. How could he be so blind, so criminally ungrateful? Of course his saints had been helping him. It was not thanks to his own efforts alone that he was still alive. Throughout all his desperate ducking and diving beneath the waves his survival had depended upon something utterly beyond his control, the grip on his ankles so resolutely maintained by the other man in the raft. Time after time he had been held securely, at God knows what cost in pain and determination, by, of all men, Epifanio, the man he had believed to be hell-bent on killing him.

He looked across at the shabby scarecrow lying slumped and exhausted against the far wall of the raft; he saw the head lolling, the arms dangling limply, the legs swollen, festering and seeping with blood and pus – and he realized that here was a miracle indeed. How it must have hurt Epifanio, what agony it must have been for him to kneel on those hideously wounded legs, what temptation there must have been as he rocked back and forth in the filth, to release his grip and free himself from torment. Yet Epifanio, tenaciously and heroically, had held on.

The saints had produced their answer. Imeldo now saw with heart-piercing clarity that he had been saved not only from drowning, but from the soul-destroying suspicions that had brought him to the very point of contemplating murder in imagined self-defence. He saw, too, that responsibility was now back in human hands, in his hands, and he shouted almost cheerfully to Epifanio as he once again pulled the surgical scissors from his waistband.

'You were great, really great – and now I'm going to reward you by stealing half your blanket.'

Stifling Epifanio's rising protest with a laugh, he explained, as he laboriously cut away a sizeable section of the plastic sheet, 'There's still plenty left, enough for shelter and enough to catch rainfall if we ever get the chance. But right now, Epifanio, I need your help just one more time. I'm sorry, for it'll probably hurt like hell – but this bit of sheeting may save our necks.'

And so once again Epifanio anchored his companion's legs and once again Imeldo went duck-diving under the raft. It was gruelling, agonizing work for both of them, but at the end of it all the raft once more had a bottom to it, a square of plastic tucked and roughly secured beneath the ropes that were binding the whole fragile contraption together.

It was nightfall before the work was done, and as the two men sank back exhausted Imeldo produced not only a biscuit and a can of water, but also the nugget of hope and encouragement he had been hugging to himself all day, preserving it for just such a moment as this, when Epifanio richly deserved some reward and when, for once, he was in the right frame of mind to appreciate it.

'Epifanio, d'you realize what day it is? This is the fifth of January, the day we were due to reach Japan. It's a whole week since we went down, and so far we've seen nobody, but now the search will really be stepped up. Every damned ship and aeroplane in the Pacific will be out looking for us. You'll see, another day, two at the most, and we'll be on our way home.'

His enthusiasm was infectious, and for once Epifanio allowed himself to share a few minutes of optimism. 'Yes. It'll soon be over. They should have found us before now, but now they'll make certain of it.'

The two men grinned at each other in sudden brief friendship. It was as well for their morale that they were unaware that on 5 January 1976, seven days after the *Berge Istra* had exploded and sunk, killing all but two of her crew, her owners, Sig. Bergesen, had not even informed her insurers at Lloyds nor alerted the rescue services to the effect that she was missing.

Chapter Eleven

SIG. BERGESEN'S FAILURE to report anything amiss with the *Berge Istra*, even when no word had been heard from her for over a week, was not the only puzzling component of the communications pattern established during her final voyage, a pattern that on investigation revealed several surprising departures from normal procedure.

On earlier journeys Captain Hemnes had always made use of a maritime service operated under the control of the United States Coast Guard. This service, AMVER (Automated Mutual Vessel Emergency Rescue), receives coded messages from ships at sea reporting their position, changes of course, alterations of speed or other significant data, and operates twenty-four hours a day. Such messages are fed into a computer, and should any participating vessel send out an SOS signal, the AMVER centre, receiving it automatically, will pinpoint its position and immediately summon all nearby shipping to the rescue.

No such message, indeed no message at all was received by AMVER from the *Berge Istra* during the entire final voyage, and no explanation of such unaccustomed silence was demanded or offered by the subsequent Liberian Board of Investigation, who dismissed this extraordinary departure from normal procedure in a few casual words. 'The reasons for the *Berge Istra* having failed to participate in the [AMVER] system during its last voyage must remain for ever a mystery.' No one, seemingly, thought it politic to ask a simple supplementary question: why must they? The owners, surely, must have known the answer, for not even the captain of a ship has the authority to introduce a major alteration in standard procedure without consulting or at least informing his employers.

Although AMVER thus remained ignorant of the *Istra*'s position and progress, that ignorance was not shared by Sig. Bergesen, for they and Captain Hemnes had conducted almost daily ship-to-shore conversations through an entirely different medium, the Norwegian Rogaland Radio. The frequency of these contacts during the period leading up to the disaster would seem to suggest that the owners and master had much to discuss, for it made a striking contrast to their usual communications procedure whereby the *Istra* would merely contact headquarters every Wednesday as a simple matter of routine. These conversations, which were recorded, in fact related to Captain Hemnes' growing concern over the deteriorating mechanical condition of his ship. Yet this almost daily link cannot be regarded as a sensible precaution against sudden emergency, for in the area through which the *Istra* was sailing Rogaland Radio, unlike AMVER with its round-the-clock service, operated for only six hours out of each twenty-four.

The last Rogaland contact between the *Istra* and her owners was made at 13.58 hours GMT on 28 December 1975, just two days before the sinking, and on that same day the radio officer, Michael LeMarche, also telephoned home.

LeMarche was an outstanding young man who had forged a remarkable and enviable life-style during his thirty-four years. On graduation from Radio School in Bridlington he had joined Marconi, sailed for Buenos Aires on his very first voyage, and never looked back. On great liners and on banana boats he had travelled the world, gained all manner of experience both personal and professional, and steadily established a reputation as a highly competent, obviously talented, and extremely likeable ship's officer.

On shore in Warminster he had met and married Sandra, the daughter of a local bank manager, and between them they determined to share all the opportunity for adventure his profession had to offer, to live their life to the full. They had sailed together on big ships when Sandra gave up her on-shore employment to sign on as a stewardess, and they had pottered about in dinghies and small sailers around the Channel Islands, Michael's place of birth and his spiritual home.

When their son was born they decided to put down roots for the future. Michael bought a plot of land and began building a bungalow on his beloved Alderney, but to pay for it he carried on, for the time being, with his career as a radio officer. Soon, however, he and Sandra had formulated their Great Plan for the future, and their first step towards bringing it to life involved a visit to Norway. Both of them loved that country and its people, and as Michael spoke Norwegian with the fluency of a native they had no shortage of friends to help them in their quest and before long they found and purchased a fishing-boat. Having bought it, they sailed it together across the Skagerrak, along the coasts of Germany and France, and over to Alderney, where they meant, eventually, to go into the 'shipping' business on their own account.

All this was the subject of excited discussion between Michael and Sandra, who was spending the Christmas holidays with his parents, when he made his last call to her on 28 December 1975. He talked, too, with his mother and stepfather, and persuaded them, when this voyage was completed, to transport their trailer-caravan over to Norway and let Sandra and himself guide them on a tour of that incomparably beautiful country.

The future looked wonderful to Michael LeMarche at the end of 1975, and his last message to his wife and parents was that the ship was sailing uneventfully, in perfect weather, towards arrival in Kimitsu only one week hence. Two days after making that call he died with his crew and captain in the inferno that engulfed the *Berge Istra*. What happened then happened so fast that even he, a supremely efficient radio officer, could not find the seconds needed to send out a call for help.

Such a call, or even the neglected link with *AMVER*, would not, of course, have saved the *Istra* or the lives of the thirty men and women who went down with her, but an SOS of one sort or another, notifying the rescue services of the disaster, might well have saved Imeldo Barreto Léon and Epifanio Perdomo López from the prolonged torture that, had they but known it, on 5 January 1976 was only just beginning. The current bearing them away from the scene of the explosion was running at no more than two knots, and an aircraft sent out immediately on AMVER's information could scarcely have failed to find them. But AMVER, on this occasion, had no such information.

All this, happily for their sanity, was unknown to Imeldo and Epifanio as they crouched together that night in unaccustomed amity, and their thoughts were already centred on the following day, 6 January. For to a Spaniard, and most of all to a Spanish father of young children, 6 January is a very special day indeed.

Chapter Twelve

THE FEAST OF EPIPHANY ON 6 January means to Spanish children what Christmas means to their counterparts in Britain and the United States. It means rising before daybreak to discover whether dreams have come true and if some longed-for presents are waiting for them as rewards, theoretically at least, for good behaviour throughout the year.

In Spain and the Canary Islands the youngsters, instead of hanging up stockings, will have placed their shoes overnight on the windowsill, and the gifts will have come not from Santa Claus but from the Magi – Caspar, Melchior and Balthazar, the three Kings of Orient – but the morning's excitement will have been the same.

'I wonder, Epifanio, what today will bring our wives and children. Will they be thinking of us almost on our way home – or will this be the day they're told we'll not be coming home again, ever?'

Epifanio had no doubts, and the tears streamed down his cheeks as he answered. 'They'll have been told. It's more than a week since the ship went down, and now she's well overdue in port. The owners must know she's gone, and I'm beginning to wonder if they've even bothered to look for us. No, our families will be mourning for us and wondering if we're in a shark's belly or lying at the bottom of the sea. God, I almost wish we were – no, no I don't, that's not true at all. I'd give anything to get out of here. I'd gladly have both arms and legs cut off, even if it meant my children had to feed me and I had to beg in the street. If we could only reach an island I'd fight wild animals with my bare hands . . .'

Epifanio's voice was rising hysterically, and once again Imeldo felt fear as the words came tumbling out. 'It isn't fair. Oh, I know I owe God a death, but why should He claim it like this? Why, if He has mercy, weren't we allowed to die quickly like the others?'

For once Imeldo felt no anger, only pity. It seemed a miracle, in truth, that Epifanio was still alive – for all his selfishness and for all his childish complaining, the man's stamina and endurance was phenomenal, almost beyond belief. He had bled copiously and he had spent a week of hellish discomfort virtually without nourishment. Not only the stench but the sight of his ugly, suppurating legs told of the pain he must be suffering and, unnoticed until now by Imeldo, a new obscenity had been added to his torment. For days he had been lying on the rusted screws of the broken weather-hood and now, as he rolled about in his anguish, his back was exposed to Imeldo's horrified gaze.

Criss-crossed, from shoulder to waistline, a pattern of deep, fiery, red and purple weals marked and tortured Epifanio like an old-fashioned victim of the lash. No, vowed Imeldo, no matter how badly this lacerated skeleton of a man might behave, he could not wholly be blamed.

For the rest of that dreadful feast day of Epiphany, until darkness came not as a danger but as a relief, Imeldo forced himself to ignore his companion's stream of accusations, threats and complaints and he himself spoke only once, again at nightfall.

'Here, Epifanio, have a quarter of a biscuit, and let me wet your lips with my fingers. We've got to halve the rations, and the water's almost gone.'

* * *

The next two days, 7 and 8 January, were to remain linked together in the memories of both survivors, for they started with a splash, spanned forty-eight hours of unbroken anxiety over yet another fresh hazard, and ended with a sigh of relief and a renewed determination, at least on Imeldo's part, to accept that God seemed to be on their side and it was up to themselves to help Him along.

The splash, loud enough to attract their attention despite the continued battering of the storm, signalled the arrival of a terrifying threat which took the form of a seven-foot swordfish, a powerful, muscular, self-propelling torpedo with a gruesome, sharply serrated blade protruding from its blunt black snout, a blade that could rip both men and platform to rags and tatters with one single, scything sweep. The swordfish holds an almost mystical place in Spanish legends of the sea, and Imeldo and Epifanio clung together as the huge fish, for hour after hour, circled so close to the raft that at times they could almost have reached over to stroke its glistening back.

'That monster,' shuddered Epifanio, burying his head in a fold of plastic sheeting, 'is eyeing us, and any minute he's going to eat us up. I can't bear to watch, Imeldo, tell me when it's gone.'

'It's not likely to go. It's probably attracted by the rotting, putrid smell from these legs of yours. If only you'd let me treat them, clean them up, you wouldn't stink like a pile of wet garbage and that brute wouldn't be following us now.'

Epifanio made no answer, and did not emerge from his hideaway until the next morning, when his first sight was of Imeldo silently watching the swordfish as it continued its endless, menacing encirclement of the raft.

'Well, Epifanio, that perfume of yours seems to be damned attractive to someone, and this fellow is beginning to frighten me. You were wrong about one thing, by the way – he won't eat us, he's not a bloody shark – but he may take a run at us or he may jump right in beside us, and then God help us. He'd either cut us into slices or crush us to a pulp. To be honest, I'd rather he was a shark. If they take you, they take you quick and clean.'

This sudden outburst, so unlike the Imeldo of old, touched some hidden spring in the complex mechanism of his companion's mind, and at once Epifanio effortlessly, and probably quite subconsciously, began to display a new facet of his strange and unpredictable personality. He sought refuge from his fear in fairy-tale fantasy, in the magical imagination of a child.

'Perhaps you're right about the perfume, Imeldo. D'you know, I believe that the swordfish really loves us. I swear he spent the whole night right under the raft. I could sense him, almost feel him swimming around beneath me, keeping me company. Maybe he's been sent to watch over us, not to harm us. Oh, if we could only tie a rope around his waist, he could pull the raft and us with it all the way to safety, perhaps even . . . who knows . . . all the way home.'

Both men, by now, must have been light-headed from their week-long ordeal, for amazingly the placid, practical, unimaginative Imeldo found such solace in this nonsense that he too began to fabricate scenarios of wildly impossible rescues and almost to believe, moreover, that they might come to pass.

But as the sun went down on the evening of 8 January, the curtains of consciousness parted again to reveal harsh reality and each of these reluctant partners turned once more to his own primary source of comfort and hope for the future. Epifanio renewed his prayers to the Virgin of the Snows, Imeldo deliberated how best he might catch fish to feed them as soon as the storm showed the very first sign of dying down.

And unknown to either of them, many thousands of miles

away in London, the world was being made aware that one of the largest vessels ever launched, the *Berge Istra*, was missing under circumstances that would soon send the world's media scurrying to their typewriters, cameras and microphones. Here was mystery; here, they hoped, was news.

Chapter Thirteen

Oslo, Jan. 7 – Managers of ore/oil motor vessel Berge Istra reported today that vessel loaded 188,000 tons of iron ore at Tubarao and left Nov. 29 for Kimitsu, E.T.A. Jan. 5, but not arrived yet. Thirty-two persons on board including thirteen Norwegian officers.

LACONIC BUT NONETHELESS ALARMING, this announcement in Lloyd's Weekly Casualty Report stirred up brisk activity in organizations and offices around the world, and anxious men of widely differing backgrounds and professions began posing questions that were to be asked many times during the weeks and months ahead, but never answered.

Why had Captain Hemnes, foregoing his usual practice, made no use on this voyage of the AMVER rescue service? And why had Sig. Bergesen, the ship's owners, remained silent for more than a week, despite the fact that as early as 30 December the *Berge Istra* had failed to make a routine radio report? The last word heard from her by anyone had been a brief message through Nagasaki Radio, passed at 19.24 hours on 29 December, reporting her position as latitude 01 14N, longitude 126 56E, a reading that placed her some 174 miles south west of Mindanao Island in the Philippines.

Once Sig. Bergesen did put out calls for assistance, top of their list of priorities was the request that search operations be initiated by various services and authorities in the Pacific area. From Australia, the Philippines, Indonesia, and Japan, and above all from the United States of America, the response was immediate – and massive. The first to deal with the problem, on 7 January, were the Americans via the United States Pacific Rescue Adjustment Headquarters in San Francisco. A call by them to the Japanese Maritime Safety Agency in Tokyo led to aerial reconnaissance flights by aircraft of the Japanese Coast Guard, and to a series of radio broadcasts passing look-out instructions to every vessel afloat in the south west Pacific.

On the same day, the 18th Tactical Fighter Wing/Rescue Coordination Center (RCC) of the United States Air Force was asked by the United States Coast Guard to be the Search Mission Coordinator, and at 19.50 hours that evening they accepted the responsibility. Early next morning the RCC went to work.

'We started,' says Sgt Richard Thomson, the NCO Controller on duty that day, 'by initiating an extended communications search. We alerted other RCCs in Tokyo, Guam, and the Philippines, and we checked out every port or harbour along the *Istra*'s route to find out if anyone had heard from her. We made an all-ships radio broadcast asking for sightings of wreckage, of survivors, or naturally of the ship herself. All day long the reports kept coming in, and each and every one of them was negative.'

That evening at the core of the whole operation, the Rescue Coordination Center at Kadena, Japan, plans were made and orders issued to the USAF aircrew commanders for the launching, at first light on Friday 9 January 1976, of what was to become the biggest, most technically comprehensive, and far-reaching search mission in the history of Air Sea Rescue.

First to take off, at dawn, was Captain Ronald Wojack, USAF, piloting a Hercules HC-130. This was no ordinary aircraft, it was one of several assigned to the 33rd Aerospace Rescue and Recovery Squadron USAF since 7 November 1972, and it embodied a number of modifications making it significantly different from the run-of-the-mill Hercules, the C-130. Captain Wojack's aircraft had two internal 1,800 gallon fuel tanks, it could fly for 7,000 miles on one sortie, and it could stay in the air for sixteen hours. It could muster a speed of 350 mph, and if necessary it had the ability to refuel in mid-air, so enabling it to continue its search. Its scientific equipment included not only special electronic instruments for controlling search and recovery operations, but also a top secret flare-launcher that allowed such operations to be carried out successfully even after dark. If any aircraft, concentrating during this initial sortie on the area from which the *Istra* had sent her last signal, if any aircraft were to solve the mystery of her disappearance, this modern marvel was surely the one.

But it was not to be and for one member of the Hercules' crew, at least, the failure to discover anything was bitterly disappointing. Sgt Harold Burded, a radar scanner aboard the HC-130, reported sadly: 'This was my first mission. I'd never have believed a big ship like that would be so hard to find – but all we ever saw was miles and miles of water.'

Just how hard it is to find even the biggest ship in an ocean as vast as the Pacific was already well known to some of those most closely concerned with the fate of the *Berge Istra*. The owners Sig. Bergesen and the members of the syndicates in London and Oslo who had risked the loss of millions to insure her were all well aware of the difficulties, for this was not the first time in her short life that the *Istra* had encountered serious problems at sea, nor the first time they had suffered acute anxiety as a result. In 1974, only two years after she had been built at the Uljanik Shipyard in Pula, Yugoslavia, the vessel had 'gone missing' during a voyage in Far Eastern waters, and the incident had caused a brief flutter of dismay amongst Norwegian Insurance underwriters who were already suffering heavily as new large tankers and combination carriers were added to the national commercial fleet. For although the number of major casualties amongst Norwegian vessels had remained more or less constant, the cost of these losses had rocketed. In 1972 the amount paid out in insurance had been 1.7 million dollars; in 1973 the decimal point had disappeared and the figure read 17 million. By 1974 it had soared to 28 million dollars. Small wonder the underwriters had held their breath on that earlier occasion as they waited for news of the missing vessel. Their suffering had started when she had failed to make a routine radio contact or to respond to their calls, and it had continued for four days and nights of silence as the *Berge Istra* drifted disabled somewhere south-east of Okinawa.

But that period of shore-based anxiety had lasted for only four days, and it had ended with good news. Now, in the first days of 1976, the waiting had already lasted twice that time and more, and amongst the owners and insurers even the most optimistic must have begun to allow at least the possibility of a major disaster.

A faint ray of hope arose on 8 January with the news from Canberra, Australia that garbled and unexplained signals possibly relating to the *Istra* had been received by two radio stations, Broome and Singapore. Broome, it transpired, had heard what they described as 'an auto-alarm sounding through static' at 21.30 hours GMT on 3 January. Singapore had reported receiving Mayday distress signals at 20.40 hours and 21.00 hours GMT on the same date, but intelligibility had been very poor and no response had been possible. Later signals according to Singapore had sounded as if a position were being given, and one moment of clarity had produced the words 'eleven crew members missing. Life boat only . . .'

This information had been relayed by the two radio stations to the Marine Operations Centre in Canberra, but as no further signals had been received during the hours of darkness the MOC took no direct action, leaving it to base stations to listen out for any more Mayday calls that might be sent. The ray of hope had been faint indeed, and it vanished altogether on 9 January when the *Istra*'s owners were informed that the distress signals had in fact come from the East German motor vessel *Capella*, which later sank in the North Sea.

Japanese boats continued to make surface searches and Japanese, American and Australian aircraft carried on with their aerial patrols, but the first few days of the rescue operation yielded not one single piece of valuable information. Such reports as did come in were depressing, and those waiting were not cheered by an announcement from the Meteorological Agency in Tokyo that the weather had been bad when the *Berge Istra* lost ship-to-shore contact, and that a tropical storm was located in the area where she had disappeared. What was most worrying of all to marine technical experts, however, was the thought that such a huge vessel, weighted well down on her load-line and therefore in what is termed a 'sea kindly' condition, could vanish without any trace.

Back in Tenerife, and especially in the busy *barrios* of Taco and El Cardenal where most of the *Berge Istra*'s seamen had their homes, the torment caused by the belated announcement from Oslo was more personal. Some of the wives and families surrendered immediately to despair. Others clung to the belief that the *Istra*, as they had been repeatedly assured, was unsinkable – few of these, presumably, had ever heard of the *Titanic*.

But for the two men at the heart of it all, for Imeldo and Epifanio, there was nothing at all to think about but the certainty that help was not yet at hand and they must continue to face life together alone on the raft.

Chapter Fourteen

THE STRANGE DICHOTOMY of their relationship, each man alone in himself yet bound inescapably to the other, grew more pronounced as each day and night dragged endlessly on. With almost any other man he had ever known, thought Imeldo, even with someone he had never known, he could have forged some sort of bond. They might have bolstered each other's courage when it seemed to be ebbing, lifted each other's spirits when they flagged. They might even have talked, sometimes, of pleasant, cheerful things, good times past and still better times ahead.

But such a partnership with Epifanio? Not for one moment could he even dream it possible; never had he known a less generous-spirited creature, nor experienced a relationship so barren and so totally one-sided. Far from drawing comfort from Epifanio's presence, Imeldo found ease of mind only when his companion had slunk growling beneath his plastic covers, and the strain was beginning to tell on his nerves.

He no longer sought to start conversations. He approached Epifanio only when necessary, to cover him if the plastic flapped free in the wind, to lend a hand as he struggled in search of comfort and, with decreasing frequency, to offer a morsel of biscuit or a tiny sip of brackish water from the can he held out habitually to catch what he could of the driving rain. He expected no word of thanks, and was glad when none came. Let Epifanio call as loud as he liked upon his Lady of the Snows; he, Imeldo, would hold himself together like a man and seek salvation by keeping his hands busy and his mind concentrated upon matters of immediate, practical importance.

In this resolve, with so little help available, Imeldo found no great difficulty in reaching the obvious, indeed the only conclusion – their future, if they were to have one, lay in fish. Here they were, the pair of them, starving in the middle of a whole ocean of natural nourishment. Yet he had hooks, he had lines, and most of his life, for God's sake, he had been a professional fisherman earning his living from the sea. How in Heaven's name could he have been so blind, so full of fear that he could not even think? Now, just let this storm die down, these seas flatten out so he could cast a line, run it through his practised fingers, feel its movements and its changing tension . . .

'Epifanio – get your head out of that sack. We're going to be all right, all right, I tell you! As soon as this damn wind drops we're going to be eating again, and then all we'll need is a drop of rain coming down on us instead of across, so we can catch it and store it. When the wind drops you'll have all the food you can eat.'

This sudden boisterous optimism on the part of Imeldo, and Epifanio's response to it, was leading inexorably, like a fuse first smouldering, then sputtering, towards a point where the two men's growing hatred of each other was in danger of destroying them both.

'Oh yes, and what sort of food will that be?'

'Fish, man, fish – they're swimming all around us, and just as soon as I can get at them, Epifanio, I can catch them.'

Imeldo's eyes were bright with excitement, his heart full to bursting with this new promise of survival and the pride in knowing that it would be his skills, his experience, his endeavour that would surely bring them both through.

The sneer on Epifanio's face was ugly with contempt. 'Oh yes – very nice. But how the hell are we going to cook them?'

Imeldo stared at him, scarcely believing. 'Cook them? Are you crazy? We eat them as we catch them.'

'Not as crazy as you are if you think I'm going to eat raw fish. God Almighty, and you complain about me and my legs – I tell you it's you, Imeldo, you're the one that's disgusting.'

A vein at the side of Imeldo's forehead began to throb, and a slow trickle of ice-cold sweat crawled down the side of his temple.

'I'm disgusting, am I? Do you know what disgust is, you filthy, ungrateful bastard? Disgust's what I felt every time I put my mouth to yours and sucked in the stink from your rotten bowels – you were shitting upwards, and I went on tasting it, and spitting it out and retching over it for days. Even when I dipped my hand in the water and wiped my mouth, it was my hand that got dirty and not my lips that got clean. And you just lay there hour after hour complaining. Not even a mother would have done for you what I did, but from you, you selfish sod, I get not one word of thanks. And now, after I've just told you how I'm going to save your worthless bloody life, what do you do? Tell me I'm disgusting because I'm offering something not quite up to your fastidious fucking standards.'

For once, in the face of such loathing, such cold, deep-rooted anger, it was Epifanio who was rendered speechless.

The two men sat glaring at each other in silence as the sun went down on the evening of 9 January, whilst, far away and unknown to them, after a day of fruitless searching, the aircraft of several countries flew back to their bases empty-handed.

Chapter Fifteen

IF SUCH LACK OF SUCCESS brought only frustration to those involved in the search operation, to the media it came as a Godsend. In both hemispheres newspaper, radio, and television editors assigned teams of reporters to follow up each item of news or non-news as it came over on the wire-service or in Lloyd's Intelligence Reports. The less hidebound journals had no qualms about setting their feature writers and more sensation-minded sub-editors loose upon the story. The *Daily Mirror*, on 9 January, headlined its item 'RIDDLE OF THE LOST SUPER-TANKER' and larded the copy with clichés such as 'Mystery last night shrouded the fate of . . .' and 'vanished without trace with her thirty-two-man crew'. Even *The Times*, on 10 January, went so far as to use a term usually associated with crime reports or detective fiction: 'The only clue to the fate of the carrier is that a typhoon passed through the area at about the time of the last message.'

In other papers around the world dark references were made to the Bermuda Triangle, and the more knowledgeable among the journalists concerned, or those who had done their research, pointed out that south-east of Japan lay another mystery zone that might prove more relevant to the disappearance of the *Berge Istra*. In a book, called *The Bermuda Triangle* by Charles Berlitz (Granada Publishing 1975), which at the time had only recently been published, the author, a distinguished commentator on the world's great mysteries, had written:

'Investigators of the Bermuda Triangle have long noted the existence of another mystery area in the world's oceans, southeast of Japan, between Japan and the Bonin Islands, specifically between Iwo Jima and Marcus Island, with a record and reputation indicative of special danger to ships and planes. Whether the ships have been lost from underwater volcanoes or sudden tidal waves, this area, often called the Devil's Sea, enjoys at least officially an even more sinister reputation than the Bermuda Triangle in that the Japanese authorities have proclaimed it a danger zone. This action came about after an investigation carried out by Japanese surface craft in 1955.

'The Devil's Sea had long been dreaded by fishermen, who believed it was inhabited by devils, demons, and monsters which seized ships of the unwary. Aircraft and boats had disappeared in the area over a period of many years, but during the time when Japan was at peace, nine modern ships disappeared in the period of 1950 to 1954, with crews totalling several hundred persons, in circumstances characteristic (extensive air-sea searches, lack of wreckage or oil slicks) of the happenings in the Bermuda Triangle.

'The Bermuda Triangle and the Devil's Sea share a striking coincidence. The Bermuda Triangle includes, almost at its western terminus, longitude 80 west, a line where true north and magnetic north become aligned with no compass variation to be calculated. And this same 80 W changes its designation when it passes the poles, becoming 150 E. From the North Pole south, it continues on, passing east of Japan, and crosses the middle of the Devil's Sea. At this point in the center of the Devil's Sea, a compass needle will also point to true north and magnetic north at the same time, just as it does at the western border of the Bermuda Triangle on the other side of the world.

'The unexplained losses in this Japanese equivalent of the Bermuda Triangle were instrumental in inspiring a government-sponsored investigation of the area, which took place in 1955. This expedition, with scientists taking data as their ship, *Kaiyo Maru No. 5*, cruised the Devil's Sea, ended on a rather spectacular note – the survey ship suddenly vanished with its crew and the investigating scientists!'

Before dismissing the newspaper and radio reporters' references to such possible explanations as fanciful or sensational journalese it may be worth noting that Denzil Stuart, writing in *Lloyd's List*, no less, the Bible of maritime commerce, remarked that 'The *Berge Istra* has all the ingredients of a classic mystery of the sea.' If the *List* saw things thus, who could blame a daily writer in the popular press for allusions ranging from the Bermuda Triangle to the *Marie Celeste*? As flight after flight by reconnaissance aircraft found nothing, not even an oil slick, to indicate the fate or whereabouts of a vessel weighing over a quarter of a million tons, there was nothing but speculation to fill the page.

For Imeldo and Epifanio, however, conditions deteriorated yet further. By 9 January, after yet another night of brooding and bitterness, Epifanio had sufficiently recovered from the shock of Imeldo's tirade to resume his attacks over the sharing of their meagre rations.

'Funny, isn't it, the way the water and biscuits are always kept in your corner, eh Imeldo? I know what you're up to, you sod. You're stealing food behind my back, eating a whole biscuit to my half and drinking whenever you feel like it. You're hoping I'll die so you can have the lot, and you think you're getting away with it because I can't move about. Well from now on you put the stuff between us where we can both reach it.'

'Oh sure – and watch every damn thing we've got go down

your gullet in one gulp? Not bloody likely. Pretty soon, anyway, we'll have all the food we can eat. Christ, I don't fancy raw fish either, but they tell me the Japs eat it all the time, and at least it'll keep us alive.'

'You can eat all the fish you can catch, stuff yourself with it, grow fat on it for all I care – then I can have what's left of the biscuits. That's only fair. You may be able to stomach uncooked fish, but I can't – I'm not a bloody animal.'

'No, you're a greedy, gutless, self-centred bastard of a man, and I'm sick of the sight of you. I've fed you, cleaned you, kept you alive, and then listened to you calling me a thief. Now you can listen to me, because I mean every last word of what I'm about to say. If I hear any more about you having all the biscuits, I won't give you any at all, you hear me? And . . .' Imeldo leaned forward, waiting, forcing Epifanio to meet his stony stare, 'if you make just one more attempt to grab the rations while I'm dividing them – just one more – I swear to God I'll throw you right over the side.'

Epifanio, probably wisely, decided to believe him, and it was two tacitly-acknowledged enemies who went nervously to sleep that night.

Chapter Sixteen

THE TYPHOON FINALLY BLEW ITSELF OUT during the hours of darkness, and on the morning of 10 January Imeldo and Epifanio awoke bewildered to calm seas and a soft breeze. No longer pitching and tumbling, battered by huge waves and thrown from ramparts to dungeon by howling winds, the raft was drifting quietly on the equatorial counter-current, gliding eastwards towards the promise of the rising sun.

Imeldo, without speaking, untied the ropes that had secured his companion throughout the storm and busied himself in tidying up the raft. He coiled ropes, folded the plastic sheeting, sorted out the fishing tackle, stowed the biscuits, bandages and water-cans – now empty and useful only for catchment – and baled what he could of the slopping oil and water from around their ankles. Perfect drainage was impossible, and a small soggy puddle of blood and filth remained as an ugly reminder of all they had been through. But there was order, and since the polystyrene sides of the raft were no longer wet, he revelled in the luxury of stripping off his sodden vest and trousers and watching them dry in the sun.

Epifanio was the first to break the long silence, typically with a complaint.

'Now the wind drops, now the bloody sun comes out, now that it's too late and we're going to die anyway. The biscuits are nearly gone thanks to your thieving, and I'll not last beyond tomorrow. Well you know what? I don't fucking care, honest to Christ I don't – I've suffered enough and I'll be glad when it's all over. In fact I'm ready to throw myself overboard and right now.'

Imeldo had had enough. 'Go ahead then, but for Christ's sake do it quietly and don't make a splash – I'm trying to catch fish.'

Imeldo was in his element now. He had of course no bait, but a rummage through the raft's survival pack had produced a very serviceable substitute in the form of two spoon rigs, curved slivers of silver plating that would dance on the line, glint and shimmer as the sun's rays struck the water. Trawled close to the surface and manipulated with care they would surely provide a lure too tempting for a fish far out in the Pacific waters and unused to the wiles of men to resist? But there were only two spoon rigs and Imeldo, threading nylon through the first of them, tied and double-checked the knots more painstakingly and securely than he had ever done before in all his forty years. Then gently, and with a murmured prayer to the Virgin of Candelaria, he slid the line over the side and into the water.

Epifanio looked long and hard at him in silent and undisguised disgust. Then, still without a word, he unfurled the plastic sheeting that Imeldo had folded, wrapped it around himself and, once again, despite the sunshine and the sudden freedom from immediate danger, burrowed down into his own dark and fear-ridden world, eyes and mind clenched tight against reality.

All day Imeldo sat there, now teasing the line to make the spoon rig jump, now letting it trail lazily behind the raft, the lure turning gently with the movements of the sea, but always with a knowledgeable forefinger held against the run of the nylon thread, sensitive and ready for the sudden convulsive jerk that would spell success. No such triumph was to come on this first sortie, but long years as a fisherman had schooled him in both patience and optimism, and the familiar activity was in itself a soothing distraction from his increasing anxiety as to the mental and emotional stability of his companion Epifanio. Surely it wasn't natural, he mused, for a grown man, a father of children, to be so afraid of the world around him that he physically hid himself from it? And not just any grown man, but of all people, Epifanio – Epifanio the braggart, the self-styled desperado of dockland, the wild and witty hero of a thousand improbable adventures, the gay galliard who could charm the drawers off the women and scare the wits out of the men? Imeldo puzzled over the strangeness of it, but could never have imagined that very soon something as innocent as his attempts at fishing would goad Epifanio to such blind fury that the truth of his emotional trauma – or something close to the truth, for with Epifanio one could never be quite certain – would come tumbling from his lips in a cascade of anger that very evening.

The outburst came as the sun was setting and Epifanio, peering from beneath his coverings, sensed that it was time for the evening meal. He emerged from the darkness, where he had lain for hours wallowing in self-pity and resentment, with an evil temper already rising. The sight of Imeldo still silently plying his line, placid and serene as if on Galilee, was simply more than he could bear. The last vestige of control fragmented, and the inner torment of Epifanio Perdomo López came pouring out, seething and destructive like lava from a volcano.

'You heartless bastard, how can you do this to me? For days you've watched me suffering, and now I'm dying of starvation right under your eyes – yet you just sit there not giving a shit, playing at your bloody hobby as if you hadn't a care in the world. How can you be such a bastard?'

Epifanio, of course, was not asking. It was no more than a

rhetorical question giving him time to draw breath before raging on. And now there was madness in his eyes.

'Have you any idea how much I'm suffering, how much I've always suffered, how my whole damned life has been misery and hell on earth? Of course you haven't.

'Do you know where I live, do you know how I live? No you don't, so I'll bloody well tell you. I live in a cave. Me, my wife and my poor bloody kids. Eight of them there are – no, it's nine now, but I've never seen the latest, he came after I'd sailed, and anyway he's what they call a mongol – not all there, you know?

'For years I watched my kids run naked and go hungry, crying for food that just wasn't there. So I came to sea, I made the sacrifice.' Imeldo winced at the hypocrisy of the man, remembering Epifanio's on-shore reputation, not all of it based upon his own boasting. 'I didn't want to come to sea, but we were living in squalor, real squalor, and that's why I became a seaman – for the money, only for the money.

'That's what I was after when I came aboard the ship. I went wild with joy when the Norwegian Consul wrote telling me I was to join her in Trinidad. Here was me – would you believe it? – being flown like a bloody millionaire to the Caribbean, me who couldn't even feed his own wife and kids. Well now, I thought, things are going to be different, so damn different.

'Then I found myself aboard the *Istra*. Can you imagine what it was like for me, who'd never been on the water, didn't know one end of the fucking boat from the other? It was so huge and so strange I kept getting lost, couldn't even find my own cabin and didn't know anyone I could ask without making a bloody fool of myself. I'd no sense of direction whatsoever, couldn't tie a knot or handle a rope, couldn't tell an oil pipe from my arsehole. So of course I landed all the dirtiest, dreariest jobs, swabbing the decks, cleaning the cabins, scrubbing out the shithouses.

'Then off duty, I'd see the other men laughing and joking together, buying coffee and whisky and beer, and I couldn't join them because I didn't know them and anyway I was sending home almost all my pay. When the men started drinking and mucking in together I'd just sort of turn away so they couldn't see my face.

'So there's no need for you to look so bloody superior. You may reckon I'm no use to you on this raft, but we're both going to die, so what does it matter? And what does it matter that I was trying for something worthwhile when the whole bloody world blew up on us.'

Epifanio's discourse came to an abrupt end and he once again wrapped himself up in his protective covering. Even now, when he might have won Imeldo's sympathy, his truculence destroyed any chance of friendship. The daylight ended with Imeldo still patiently fishing and searching hopefully for a smudge of smoke on the horizon.

Chapter Seventeen

ON SHORE BY THIS TIME, the search was under way, and neither cost nor effort was being spared by the nations attempting to trace the missing vessel. No one, from the owners down, was prepared at this stage to accept or even to predict that the *Berge Istra* had foundered, and what was really being sought was information as to how and where she ran into trouble, and an explanation as to why there had been no word from her in over a week.

At the Rescue Co-ordination Center in Kadena, Japan, Lt Col James Butera, USAF, commanding the 33rd Aerospace Rescue Squadron, before issuing detailed orders to his aircrews, decided to seek the advice of the one man who might be able to throw light upon the ship's probable movements and the actions to be expected from her master, Captain Hemnes. Captain Tor Gudmundsen, himself a former master of the *Berge Istra*, was already in Tokyo waiting to assume command of her for the next stage of her voyage. He responded at once to Butera's call for assistance. He drew out on the navigational charts the probable routes he thought the vessel might have followed on finding herself with a problem, and his summing-up of the situation was on the whole reassuring. He reminded the USAF authorities of the occasion in 1974 when the *Istra* had been missing and unreported for four days, and went on to say: 'It's not unlikely for a ship to miss position reports for several days when steaming in that part of the world.' Adding by way of explanation, 'Atmospheric conditions down there make radio transmission and reception very difficult and sometimes nearly impossible.'

This was a heartening opinion, and the 33rd ARS applied to the project all the considerable resources at their command. The formation to which they belonged, the 18th Tactical Fighter Wing, was within days of celebrating a Unit anniversary representing forty-nine years abroad in the service of the United States, and what could better mark the occasion than a major aerial operation that was no mere routine peacetime exercise but a genuine, grand scale air-sea-rescue assignment?

When the armed forces of the United States put their hearts and minds to meeting the demands of the moment it makes for an impressive sight. During the next eight days and nights of round-the-clock activity the aircrews under command of the 18th Tactical Fighter Wing flew fifty-one separate sorties, racking up nearly 476 hours of operational flying time, and carried out a systematic and scientific search covering 450,000 square miles of the Pacific Ocean. No air-sea rescue operation quite like it had ever been mounted before, and more than once during the first few days came moments when success seemed likely and hopes ran high, both in the aircraft and amongst those busily plotting, analysing and recording the individual search reports rolling into the operations room back at base.

On 11 January an observer in one of the search aircraft spotted a yellow cylinder floating some forty miles off Mindanao Island. 'It looked the sort of thing that might form part of the survival gear on a big ship,' he reported later, 'and every manjack in the crew was staring at the water as we swooped down on it to have a closer look. The skipper tilted us over on a wingtip and started circling, circling, wider and wider – and, Christ, you should have heard the shouting over the intercom as one after another we started spotting logs and spars and bits of broken furniture floating around in a patch of sea just a few miles away from the cylinder.'

Now, surely, they were on to something at last, and the crewmen busied themselves with their specialized tasks. The navigator calculated and recorded their exact position, the observers threw out smoke-floats and recognition-buoys to mark it for future callers, and the radio operator sent out a message announcing their find to the nearest Rescue Coordination Center, on Okinawa. The staff there, in their turn, checked the position and movements of all shipping in the area, and within an hour they had made contact with the Japanese motor ore carrier *Tobata Maru*. The captain of this vessel, acknowledging the signal, reported that he was changing course and heading towards the Philippines, and that he hoped to reach the area in which the debris had been sighted at about 23.30 hours that night. Four aircraft of the USAF and two more from the Philippines Air Force continued their aerial patrol for as long as daylight lasted, and everyone involved in the operation, on land, at sea, or in the air waited eagerly for the *Tobata Maru*'s midnight message.

Waiting forms an integral, nerve-racking part of any search and rescue operation, and during the next twenty-four hours the bulletins issued by the various agencies concerned gave small but tell-tale signs of increasing tension. Reuters, with unwonted imagery, reported that American aircraft were 'scouring the western Pacific Ocean'; United Press International announced that planes of the Philippines Air Force, in liaison with the US Rescue Co-ordination Center on Manila, were engaged on a day-long mission off the coast of Davao Province. But by the end of the day nothing of real significance had resulted from the search.

The first 'hard' news, when it came in a Reuters' announcement on 13 January, represented only continuing effort in the face of a sickening let-down for all concerned. The message read: 'Tokyo, 13 Jan. – Five American rescue planes took off from Okinawa today to search for *Berge Istra*. The US Rescue Co-ordination Center at Okinawa said that three patches of debris sighted near Mindanao had turned out to be ordinary ocean flotsam and not connected with the missing vessel.' A later report stated that 'two American aircraft were in the air this afternoon still searching for the *Berge Istra*'.

Other sources, that same day, issued equally dismal situation reports. From Okinawa it was announced that US aircraft were returning to base at nightfall with no further sightings to record. Sig. Bergesen in Oslo stated that they had no knowledge of the *Istra*'s whereabouts or condition. United Press International quoted the Maritime Safety Agency in Tokyo, which stated that, 'A joint US–Japanese air-sea search has failed to find any trace of the *Berge Istra*', and reported that a spokesman for the Agency had added the sombre forecast that, 'Unless any new development is reported by the USAF search planes, Japanese aircraft, and the Japanese patrol vessel *Izu*, will call off the search at nightfall.' The reason for this somewhat defeatist pronouncement, the spokesman went on to explain, was that although *Izu* and aircraft belonging to the Agency, as well as military planes from Okinawa, Guam, and the Philippines, had been following daily the courses of all ships in the Pacific known to be bound for Japan, not a single positive report had been filed.

The implication was depressingly obvious. In the judgement of at least one major authority on maritime safety in Far Eastern waters, the *Berge Istra* was gone for good.

Chapter Eighteen

THAT MUCH, OF COURSE, THE TWO MEN ON the raft already knew only too well. Sometimes, when their morale was at rock bottom, it seemed scarcely believable that the *Berge Istra* had ever existed, that only a few days before they had been following their trade, earning good pay, and living their lives week after week without one real worry, as they now understood the term, in the whole wide world.

Imeldo, speaking almost as much to himself as to Epifanio, broke the long silence by giving voice to the doubts and possibilities that had been turning around in his mind as he sat quietly tending his line.

'D'you know, it seems to me that maybe we're not the only ones to have got away from the ship. If you think about it, I was pretty busy for the first hour or two, and you weren't seeing or hearing a thing. Of course when the ship exploded it looked as if everything and everybody went with her – but let's face it, you and me were flying through the fucking air, paying no heed to anything whatever, all we could see was the smoke and flames. We couldn't see through them, and maybe things weren't so bad on the other side. Perhaps some of the others were sheltered from the main blast, and God knows there was plenty of escape gear aboard her apart from our raft.'

'What was there, altogether?' Epifanio, for once, sounded interested.

Imeldo, surprised and gratified by the unaccustomed

response, was glad of the chance to show off the technical expertise acquired through long service.

'Well, apart from this piddling little thing we're on there were two real rafts, big buggers meant to hold twenty men apiece, and with rations for that number.' He looked at Epifanio, but was laughing as he spoke. 'Sure, it would've been nice to have one of those, and food for twenty all to ourselves – but we haven't, so here, have a bit of biscuit and pretend it's a plate of stew.'

He carried on listing the *Istra*'s survival inventory, casting his mind back to recall every item put aboard her to save her men in an emergency. 'Those big rafts – y'know the more I think about them the more I reckon some of the others may have been lucky. You must have seen them, stacked on a platform just aft of the swimming pool. Well, they were secured there by rubber straps, which were tied to toggles on the raft . . .'

'Why?'

'Why? Because it made them automatic, self-launching if you like, that's why. When the ship sank the toggles would've ripped free and the raft would've been left floating.

'Then, of course, there were the two lifeboats. They were big bastards, built to hold fifty and each with a motor and a radio. And there was the working-boat, a sort of dressed-up dinghy. That was also fitted with survival gear. I tell you, Epifanio, I reckon there's a fair chance some of the others survived too, and were luckier than us and found an island with dusky maidens in grass skirts. That'd suit you all right, wouldn't it?'

Imeldo felt better than he had done for days, and it may have been an act of mercy that in running through the inventory of the *Istra*'s escape-and-survival gear he had completely overlooked one vital item. If he had remembered it now, and if he had mentioned it to Epifanio, the bitter irony of it might well have driven both of them beyond the limits of their mental and emotional endurance.

In the event of a sinking the captain and officers on the bridge had ready access to two portable radio beacons designed to transmit automatically a series of emergency signals when released into the sea. These were not, unfortunately, self-launching, and since no signal had been received anywhere from the *Istra* at the time of the disaster it is clear that neither the captain nor anyone else on the bridge had had a chance to throw either one of them over the side. But it was not any memory of these beacons, which were probably unknown to him, that would have brought grief to Imeldo had he thought about them now.

No, in addition to these two emergency beacons on the bridge there was a third item of electronic survival gear. There was an emergency lifeboat radio transmitter capable of sending out distress signals over many miles of ocean – and it had been stowed in the fo'c'sle head, ready to hand, right beside the tiny polystyrene life-raft that was now their home. Happily for his sanity, however, Imeldo had either never noticed it, or had by now forgotten all about it.

These various emergency transmitters had not, though, been overlooked by the men conducting the search. Told of their presence on the *Istra* by Captain Gudmundsen, the air crew commanders had clung on to their hopes and intensified their efforts. What could not be seen might yet be heard, and a radio signal is not impeded by darkness; they would work on through the night. Excerpts from a bulletin issued by the New York headquarters of the United States Coast Guard give some idea of just what this renewed enthusiasm entailed, and of how conscientiously the continuing search was carried out.

'The following areas [there comes here a long list of latitudes and longitudes] were searched electronically and visually, with a probability of detection of 90 per cent. The first two areas, designated D4 and D5, were night searches conducted on the fourth night of the operation; the remaining four areas, designated E1 to E4, were covered on the fifth day of the operation, with an additional area searched by one aircraft en route return . . .

'33 ARRS – 7 sorties for 74.6 hours. 374 TAW – 8 sorties for 85.2 hours. 54 WRS – 3 sorties for 29.4 hours. CTG 72.3 – 2 sorties for 21.6 hours. CTG 72.2 – 2 sorties for 1.8 hours. 1st SOS – 2 sorties for 17.6 hours. MSA Japan – 2 sorties for 16.9 hours. JMSDF Japan – 1 sortie for 6.8 hours. Philippine AF – 3 sorties for 6 hours. Area searched – 26,800 square miles . . .

'13 Jan. – Cumulative total 289,800 square miles in 5 days' search. A determined effort of 30 aircraft sorties and 259.9 flying hours has yielded negative results. All leads were checked out as thoroughly as possible. Numerous small and large ships have transited the search area continually, with none reporting any sightings. Not one piece of hard evidence uncovered during search.'

But on that very day – or rather, to be accurate, on that very night – came what seemed to be the breakthrough, and the shore-based waiters, watchers and aircrew commanders could scarcely contain their impatience as the hours passed towards what would surely be confirmation of good news in the morning. For one of the search aircraft, flying as low as it dared to in the darkness, had been greeted by the flash of torches as it passed over someone out there in the far reaches of the Pacific. Dawn, however, brought only heartbreak. The flyers who had spotted the torches had pinpointed their location without difficulty – and another aircraft, dispatched at first light had identified it, just as easily, as a tiny village on a tiny island. Now, in the daylight, the inhabitants, this time without the need for torches, were out in strength once again to wave greetings to the unaccustomed visitors as they roared overhead. Time after time, lower and lower, the aircraft circled, the observers straining for the sight of figures dressed in European clothes. The hopes of the crew members died within them, however, as they found themselves at last bound to accept that to this little community they themselves were the only strangers present.

It was a sad set-back, but still the American rescue teams refused to give up, and on that same day it was announced from New York that six more aircraft would take part in the operation, and the search would be switched to a new area of the Pacific covering 60,000 square miles as yet unexplored.

And somewhere in that now silent ocean, Imeldo began his serious assault upon the fish.

Chapter Nineteen

NEITHER HIS SKILLS NOR HIS PATIENCE had deserted him, and it was not long before the first inquisitive victim came nosing upwards to examine the twinkling attractions of the lure. It was a fine, fat John Dory – ten or twelve pounds if it's an ounce, said the fisherman's practised eye – and Imeldo made himself a silent promise that here was his next square meal. The fish, though, had other ideas. Time after time, swimming lazily closer, it would prod with ugly pouting lips at the glittering silver spoon rig, but never incautiously enough to swallow the hook. Instead it would glide away, so close to the surface its scales glistened in the sunlight, leaving Imeldo to swear softly and try once more, easing the line, coaxing the Dory into compliance with muttered imprecations and sweet words of love.

'Come here, my treasure, here where you'll be cherished and treated with a reverence no fish has ever known before. That's it, come closer, you slippery big bastard, before I dive in there and drag you aboard with my bare hands. Oh, you dear sweet beautiful creature – by Christ, you bugger, I can taste you now.' But for all his cursing and cajoling, the big John Dory stayed shy of the hook.

Hour after hour the grim courtship went on until even Imeldo, for all his patience and all his long experience, was almost ready to quit when suddenly the quarry came zooming recklessly to the surface, mouth gaping with greed, and the line jerked tight as the barb bit home.

'Oh dear God,' prayed Imeldo, softly letting the line run almost free, 'please, oh please don't let this nylon break.' The Dory was thrashing wildly, plenty of life was still left in him, and Imeldo felt no great faith in the unfamiliar emergency tackle packed alongside bandages and anal suppositories in the *Istra*'s survival pack. Inch by agonizing inch, he began to draw his victim closer and closer until at last, still wriggling fiercely, it was no more than a couple of feet from the rim of the raft.

'Right, you big beauty.' With one great shout, exultant yet desperate with fear of the unthinkable, Imeldo wrenched both arms violently upwards, and hoisted the glistening John Dory, a full twelve pounds of it, out of the sea, into the air and, sweeping towards him, over the low gun'le and into the raft. Panic reigned as Imeldo's prize lolloped, floundered and tossed itself hither and thither in the cramped confines of the five-foot raft. And there was total confusion and oaths fit to curdle the blood as Epifanio rose roaring from the dark seclusion of his coverings when he felt the unfamiliar body flailing against his injured legs. Imeldo, intent on somehow stunning his quarry before it could catapult itself over the side, wondered for a few frantic seconds whether he should risk losing the fish in order to quieten his nearly demented companion.

'What in the name of Christ Almighty is that?' screamed Epifanio, gazing in horrified loathing at the scaly intruder leaping from one corner of the raft to another and slapping its slithery body against each man in turn. 'It's going to hurt my legs, can't you see that? For God's sake, Imeldo, throw it out of here before it kills us both.'

'Throw it out?' Imeldo's voice rose in an incredulous shriek. 'Throw it out – have you gone fucking crazy? It's taken me a whole day of effort and a whole damn lifetime of experience to get the bastard in here. We've got food for a week here, Epifanio, and we've got it because I bloody caught it, so if you start moaning again about your fads and fucking fancies – if you start that again, you ignorant, ungrateful bastard, I swear to God I'll force-feed you, shove the stuff down your throat, backbone, scales and all.'

The uneasy, constantly changing relationship between the two survivors, though neither of them at the time realized it, was about to alter once more.

It seemed to Imeldo as if the fish would never die. Lacking a 'stunner', the short weighted mallet that had always been an essential part of his fisherman's equipment, he began clubbing the big John Dory savagely with his clenched fists. He lay across it like a wrestler to hold it safely inside the raft and he stuck his thumbs in its gills and pressed desperately, trying to choke it to death. At last it lay still but for an occasional spasm and the faint reflexive fluttering of its tail.

But how to gut it, how to cut it to pieces – how, above all, to eat it? Imeldo thought wistfully of the discarded clasp-knife, but not for long, every glimpse of Epifanio's glittering eyes and staring expression reaffirming that he was well rid of that. He would make do instead with the surgical scissors. Though small, they were sharp, and what their cutting edges could start his own strong fingers could complete.

Little did Imeldo suspect, however, that in the minutes that followed he was to come dangerously close to destroying his companion's reason entirely. Carefully, he slid the pointed blades as deeply as they would reach into the Dory's soft underbelly, and now levering, now snipping, now slicing, he ripped the big fish wide open. Plunging his hands into the Dory's gaping belly he dragged out the slithering entrails, pulled them apart and sorted through them on the raft's floor, scrabbling eagerly for the organs that would best stave off his hunger and slake his raging thirst. With nails, teeth, and scissors he tore free a slice of the liver and crammed it into his mouth, sucking and slobbering as the blood and juices spilled over his cracked lips and dribbled down his chin. Next, laughing wildly, almost demonically, he seized the blood-engorged heart of the fish and chewed it, still beating, between his teeth.

'Here,' he shouted, thrusting forward two hands full of squirming offal, 'eat your fill, Epifanio, our saints have answered us – we're saved.'

Epifanio, his eyes transfixed, his face drained of colour, crouched quivering in sheer terror, before forcing himself backwards, deep into his own corner of the raft. His hideous scream went on and on and on, reaching out to the distant horizon, far beyond sanity.

Chapter Twenty

MALUKA, HALMAHERA, OBI MAJOR, Batjan, Mindanao, Moratai and Pulao Rau. A list of the islands and their surrounding waters searched diligently by air, sea, and electronics during the feverish days and long nights of this vast, unprecedented rescue operation reads like a travelogue, but to those engaged in the search the emotion most powerfully aroused was an inner anger born of deep frustration and exacerbated by feelings of disbelief and wounded pride.

The men in the control centres, in the briefing-rooms, meteorological observatories, chart rooms, and radio and electronics stations, and those in the ships, at radar screens and echo sounders, and in the aeroplanes with their near-miraculous high technology, were professionals, professionals, moreover, suddenly presented with a once-in-a-lifetime chance to prove their skills and to demonstrate the value of them worldwide to a public who rarely even heard of them, let alone understood and appreciated their importance. Ships the size of the *Berge Istra* did not just disappear. Sure, from time to time they foundered, burned out, sank or exploded, maybe all four – but they did not simply disappear. Some sign of them had to remain – flotsam, oil, rafts, bodies. There had to be something that would enable a search team, just once, to file something more satisfying than a negative report.

As aircraft of the United States Air Force continued to fly out from Okinawa, a spokesman for the US Rescue Coordination Center at Kadena made a public statement that, though diplomatically devoid of any critical comment, just may have reflected a certain irritation on the part of the men and women actually engaged in the organization and execution of the operation. The search, said the spokesman, was now being switched to new areas, determined by current flows and weather conditions worked out by United States Coast Guard and Norwegian computers. The Co-ordination Center, he reported, had only just learned through communication with the vessel's managers that the position of the *Berge Istra* quoted on 29 December was not the location broadcast by the ship, but was a computed estimate of where she should have been, and her actual position may in fact have been 100 miles south of that location.

On the same day that this statement was issued by the Rescue Co-ordination Center at Kadena, confirming that the search was continuing, Reuters in Tokyo announced that Sig. Bergesen had stated that they had no further knowledge of the *Berge Istra* and had given her up as lost.

Imeldo, in the meantime, was steadily becoming more dependent upon his fishing tackle. Most importantly it represented a chance of survival, the difference between wavering hope and the slow certainty of death by starvation. But the threat of the latter was already over, or at least long postponed, thanks to his first catch. There were also other benefits to be derived from his skill with hook and line, however, and the effect of these was more immediate. He had no true idea of just how long the eerie caterwauling of his companion had actually lasted – long enough, God knows, and far into the night, forcing him to build his own mental refuge from reality. And so, throughout all the hours of daylight, Imeldo continued to fish. With the sea now calm and with growing confidence in the strength of his line, he became more adventurous.

As a change from the silver spoon rig he now baited his hooks with scraps of flesh from the big John Dory, and sometimes, using the spoon rig as a sinker, he would allow the lure to trail well below the surface. He found solace in using his familiar skills, and by the end of the next day, which was passed largely in silence broken only by the porcine snuffling and occasional complaint that had become Epifanio's sole communication since a dust-dry throat had at last put an end to his screeching, Imeldo had hooked, landed, killed and gutted a fine array of fish, mainly John Dorys and Dorados, and ranged them against the sides of the raft. He had food now to last the pair of them for days or even weeks – if only he could persuade Epifanio to eat, and if he could find some way to quench their thirst. Dear God, prayed Imeldo, send us just one cloud, just one little fall of rain.

No cloud appeared and no rain fell, but Imeldo was no longer the hesitant, irresolute character he had seemed for most of his life. Thirst was horrible, certainly, but it took only a little moisture to keep a man alive. God, he felt sure, would provide – but God could not reasonably be expected to deliver the goods gift-wrapped to the doorstep. Imeldo paused; God, come to think of it, had already provided. Armed with his trusty scissors and free from the baleful stare of Epifanio, huddled as usual beneath his covers, Imeldo the surgeon, the analyst, the dietician, began to dissect, to study and consider the anatomy and physiology of the fish.

His findings, based simply upon thought, observation, and plain common sense, would not have won him a university doctorate or degree – but they were sound as far as they went, and they did keep Epifanio and himself alive.

Chapter Twenty-One

'NOW LISTEN, EPIFANIO, you're going to eat, whether you like it or not.' Imeldo, his nerves stretched almost beyond endurance by the sullen, brooding silence of the past two days, pulled back a corner of his companion's protective covering and tried his best to assume a conciliatory tone as he resumed his thankless battle to save the wretched man's life.

'I've been experimenting with these fish, and honestly, when you get used to it it's not too bad. Look, I'll have a piece now and show you.' He chewed cheerfully on a chunk of liver, bravely hiding his revulsion and grinning as the blood spurted between his teeth and trickled down his jowls. 'You see? It's okay, and just a few mouthfuls will help you build up a bit of strength, if only you'll give it a chance.

'Here, try this. If you can't swallow it, at least suck it, moisten your lips, drink in some strength if you can't eat it in.' He paused, concentrating hard, forcing Epifanio to listen and to meet his eye. 'Because if you don't, then soon, very soon, you're going to die.'

He held forward a thin strip of liver, not too big, that he had carefully cut and trimmed with the surgical scissors. 'Come on now, surely this little scrap isn't too frightening for a big tough character like you. Take it in your hand, rub it across your lips and let it soften the cracks and soothe the sores. Then chew it, or if you're too timid to do that then press it, squeeze it, but for God's sake do something to get a squirt of these juices down inside you before you just dry up and wither like a broken branch. Here . . .'

Imeldo was speaking no more than the truth. In addition to his injuries, exposure, and lack of nourishment, Epifanio was by now suffering from dehydration, and it could not be very long before his bodily organs would simply cease to function. The man himself seemed to sense as much, and grudgingly he accepted the proffered slice of liver. His eyes, however, still stared accusingly at his benefactor, and Imeldo in his turn watched closely, already certain in his own mind what would happen when the slimy, bitter-tasting purple flesh touched Epifanio's fastidious lips.

He was right. The titbit had barely reached the man's mouth before it was violently rejected, thrown over the side, and Epifanio, spitting and retching, was glaring at him with all the old loathing in his eyes. Imeldo, however, was prepared for this, merely grinned amiably, produced two more ready-trimmed strips, and began to munch upon one while silently holding out the other. It was more than Epifanio could stand.

'Mother of God, but that stuff is vile. And you, you, too, are vile, crouching there grinning like a savage with the blood from that steaming gizzard running down your chin. Have you any idea what a revolting sight you make?'

Imeldo, growing wiser and more enlightened with every minute passed in this extraordinary creature's company, stared straight back at him, taking in the wasted cheeks, the glaring eyes, the skeletal rib-cage almost bursting through the sun-blackened skin, the bloated, festering, loathsome legs, and suddenly broke into laughter – not in hysteria but in genuine amusement – at the ludicrous sight of his companion fumbling irresolutely with the second strip of life-saving energy lying unasked-for in his palm. For hours to follow, silence and individual solitude returned to the raft.

This time, for Imeldo, the silence was welcome, affording him the opportunity for some serious thinking and for a realistic appraisal of the situation. Several points seemed all-important to the question of survival. First was the matter of Epifanio's shifting moods and behaviour. Certainly the man was a truculent, stubborn, disagreeable companion who was unreceptive to the power of reason. But as the tropical storm had abated, so, too, had the real violence of Epifanio's aggression, when the waves of hatred emanating from him had seemed to warn that here was a creature capable of anything. And that change had made a huge difference to Imeldo's own behaviour and attitude, not least in the matter of the meat. For the time being, at least, he was no longer afraid of Epifanio.

He was, however, afraid, very afraid for Epifanio, and his sudden awareness of this gave rise to further unaccustomed introspection. Why was he so concerned about his shipmate? Why should he care so deeply about the survival of a man for whom he had no cause, God knows, to feel either warmth or affection? Gratitude, certainly, but only for one single act of physical endurance that had benefited Epifanio no less than himself. Yes, he admired the man for the way in which he had mastered his pain to make possible the repairs to the raft – but that was not enough, surely, to outweigh all the fear he had felt, the ingratitude and verbal abuse he had suffered, and the obdurate refusal of the man beside him to make one single contribution to the dreary routine of watchfulness that might at any moment of the day or night spell the difference, for both of them, between life and death?

No, it was not enough, not nearly enough, and so slowly, as he began to look more closely than ever before into his own mind and motives, Imeldo began to realize that there were reasons beyond the altruistic for his determination that Epifanio, no matter what it might cost either of them, should remain alive. His conscious mind at last grasped what his inner self had known instinctively all along – that upon the continuing presence of Epifanio depended his own hope of survival. Epifanio might quarrel, shriek, sob or threaten, but he was there. He might retreat sulking to his coverings, but he was a living entity to be shouted at, consulted, or coaxed into eating offal even if he did not respond. He wasn't an agreeable companion, far from it, but while he still lay there breathing Imeldo could remind himself that he was not quite alone – and with that came always a flicker of hope, of faith even, a memory of other people, more dear to him by far, whom he might yet live to see, to love, and to laugh with once again.

Yes, Epifanio was important to him, and from this admission Imeldo moved on to something else, something that at first sight seemed to make no sense. He had no yearning for the return of the old Epifanio, the Epifanio who had made him throw away the clasp-knife for fear of being murdered as he slept. No, he could well do without such hours of terror – and yet. Dear God, what was he thinking of, what was he admitting to himself? Even as he asked, Imeldo knew the answer. He had no wish to die by violence or to live in fear – but he had no wish, either, to live and then die a cataleptic. Left alone, how long would it be before the numbing, unrelieved misery of total solitude and sheer despair would send him sinking into moral and mental collapse, unable to act or to think for himself, unable, at last, even to care?

He needed Epifanio, would need him as long as this ordeal should last, and – he might as well admit it – he also needed an Epifanio who would provide more stimulus, good or bad, than was coming from this sullen, defeated husk grunting and fidgeting beneath his sheet. Better the angry excitement and activity of a quarrel, better anything to send the adrenalin surging, than the demoralizing apathy into which Epifanio seemed to have sunk. No, to hell with it – he was damned if he'd give up without a fight, and he was damned if he'd let Epifanio give up either. While they still had breath, while they still had a chance, they would make what they could of it and between them, with God's good grace, they might yet pull through.

'Epifanio,' he announced brusquely, 'I'm going to tell you a story. It's a true story that I read in a magazine, and it proves at least two things. It proves that some people, even young people with half our years and a hundred times our money, can find themselves worse off than we are now, and still come through. And it proves that when a man sees Death staring him straight in the eye he will do anything to keep the monster away.'

'Jesus Christ . . .' Epifanio stuttered in fury. 'You give me the creeps. What sort of creature are you, eating raw flesh, drinking blood, talking about Death? Call him a monster? You're the monster. Just get away from me, Imeldo – just leave me alone to die in peace.'

'No, I won't leave you alone, and I won't allow you to die, because there's no need for it. And I'm going to tell you this story, and go on telling it until I'm sure you're listening. It's a true story, I promise you, not a fairy tale, and we have a lot to learn from it, you and me both.

'Not so very long ago a party of schoolboys – I think they were a college football team – were flying to or from some championships in South America, flying God knows how many thousands of feet over the Andes. Well the plane crashed, smack bang into the frozen snow and ice high up amongst the mountain peaks in some of the most God-forsaken territory in the world. They were miles from civilization, and quite a few of the crew and passengers were killed on impact.

'But not all of them. There were several survivors, though

some of them were badly hurt and soon began to die. This went on for days. They had no radio and no hope of early rescue, and before long even the strongest of them began to fade, because the food had run out and they were starving in the bitter, freezing cold.

'And do you know what they did, these schoolboys? No, don't you turn away from me, because you know, you know damn well what they did. They saw themselves dying, one after one, and so they cut up and ate their dead friends. And they survived, Epifanio, because they forced themselves to turn cannibal, to eat the flesh of their own kind, their own companions. Now the next time I offer you a slice of fish to save your life – don't you bloody dare turn your nose up because it's not being served grilled, with almonds and tomatoes.'

He was tactful enough, however, not to suggest a meal then and there, and the two of them settled down for the night wrapped in silence.

Chapter Twenty-Two

IMELDO, WAKING FIRST AS USUAL, splashed water over his face and went straight back to his battle with the fish. He found it soothing and comforting, and besides passing the time it served a purpose, because the miniature Billingsgate racked around the shallow walls of the raft meant that he could now choose what he ate. He was becoming an expert at cutting and gutting; with his little scissors he would slit each new capture from tail to top, slicing crosswise around beneath the head, and then reach into the cavity and wrench away the spine and its attachments. Then with both hands he would drag out the entrails, taking great care not to rupture the sac of bitter bile that would poison the flesh, and he would throw overboard the bones and the guts. But he would keep the head.

From each carcass and skull he would suck and chew and sometimes swallow the heart, the liver and brains, spitting the fibrous residue fastidiously over the side. When he was sure that Epifanio was not looking – for Epifanio would have considered his next act as barbarous – he would gouge out the eyes and roll them around his baking gums before chewing them, too, savouring the last tiny droplet of precious fluid lurking between the retina and the iris. Now, confident that survival was almost within their grasp, at least in terms of nutrition, he was doubly determined to persuade Epifanio to share in his discoveries. He made his preparations, and then he shook the nearest shoulder beneath the sheeting. When a scowling face glowered out at him he greeted it with a grin.

'Here, a treat for you, speciality of the house. Now don't start fussing and swearing, it isn't bloody, it isn't slimy – it isn't even raw. Here . . .'

Epifanio leaned forward, peering suspiciously at the morsel of meat thrust into his outstretched hand. Sure enough, there was no blood oozing from it, and instead of being sloppy and slithery like the liver it was reasonably firm to the touch. Unlike the liver, too, or the heart, it was not an off-putting dark purple colour. Most surprisingly of all, it felt warm, even to his calloused palm. He sniffed it warily, as if expecting it to smell of something other than fish.

'What's the catch?'

'There's no catch. I've just been doing a bit of thinking. What you've got there is a slice of the cleanest flesh from the flank, nowhere near the guts, and you've no excuse for not eating it, because it's been cooking in the sun for the past couple of hours, like in a slow oven. We're having a bloody barbecue, just like the rich *turistas* in Tenerife. So come on, Epifanio, smile and swallow it – you know you have no choice.'

It was a moment of truth for the two men, because what Imeldo was offering was not simply an encouraging invitation but also, in two quite separate senses, a challenge. The first and most obvious was that Epifanio's life now lay in his own hands – he could overcome his squeamishness, or he could watch himself die. The second challenge was to his intelligence, to his right to claim even the faintest smattering of common sense. Imeldo, tired of Epifanio's irrational ranting, had long since despaired of ever making his companion see reason. Now, however, thanks to his brainwave of laying thin strips of middle-meat along the gun'le, in effect half-curing it under the tropical sun, he was able to confront Epifanio not with words or argument but with the evidence of his own eyes and taste-buds. The rest was up to the man himself.

Like an alley-cat approaching a strange dustbin, Epifanio first sniffed at the meat as if it were poison, mauled and twisted it between his fingers and then drew it, barely touching, across his cracked and blistered lips. The saltiness made him wince, but finally, cautiously, he pushed one end of the sliver between his teeth and began to chew. His grimaces were those of a prisoner under torture, but as Imeldo watched silently, holding his breath, Epifanio persisted and at last succeeded in swallowing a few small mouthfuls of meat. For each man it was a battle fought and won, and Imeldo smiled with quiet satisfaction. Now, at last, they truly stood a chance.

He would have felt less complacent had he known that within a few hours he was to suffer one of the most horrifying experiences of his life.

Epifanio's reluctant surrender had temporarily broken down the barrier of hostility, and the rest of the morning was punctuated by snatches of desultory conversation. Not exactly friendly, for each was still nursing grievances, real or imaginary, but Epifanio for once kept his complaining in check, Imeldo recognized the effort this must have cost, and both men realized and accepted that just talking at least helped to pass the time. An onlooker, however, might have found black humour in the noontime ritual that day. Epifanio took the part of a difficult to satisfy customer and Imeldo, pathetically eager to please, the part of a fawning waiter pointing out the choicest delicacies on the *carte du jour*, fulsome in his gratitude when a recommendation was accepted and ingested. For the first time in a fortnight, both men ate what might reasonably, in comparison with previous days, have been described as a meal.

What with that, the heat of the noonday sun, and the fact that they were Spaniards, nothing could have been more natural than their subsequent dozing off into a siesta. All was peaceful until, after a couple of hours, Imeldo awoke to the call of nature and, balancing clumsily on his knees, pointed himself outwards over the shallow wall. Seconds later, and for the first time, it was Epifanio's turn to be roused from slumber by demented screaming.

'Dear Mother of God, I'm dying. I've poisoned myself, and my guts have burst open. Help me, Epifanio – for Christ's sake do something to help me before I bleed to death.'

He had half-turned towards his companion and Epifanio, lurching forward, stopped short in sheer horror. Imeldo's hands were clasped to his groin, and through his fingers, hot and steaming, came spurting an endless arc of bright crimson, glistening in the sunlight before sprinkling vermilion over the rim of the raft and the surface of the sea. Imeldo's screams were rising to a frenzy, and in that instant were sown the first seeds of a dramatic change in the relationship between these two sick and increasingly desperate men. It was a fragile thing, and slow to develop, but it was a change that was to save their lives.

'Are you hurting badly?' Epifanio's voice cut clean across his companion's hysteria, and though the tone was rasping and unsympathetic, it carried calm and authority rather than anger or fear.

Imeldo's screaming faltered and died. He knelt bewildered at the raft's edge, a puzzled, lost expression on his face as the scarlet fountain from his loins dwindled to a trickle. He fumbled, hesitant but probing, over his blood-stained lap, and his eyes were wide open as he stared across at Epifanio.

'I'm not hurting at all – I'm bleeding to death, my guts have gone, and I'm not hurting at all.'

Epifanio reached forward and put a rough hand on Imeldo's trembling shoulder. For the first time since their ordeal had begun there was a grin on his face, a chuckle in his voice.

'Of course you're not hurting – why the hell should you? That's not your blood you've been pissing, it comes from all those horrible guts you've been eating. I told you you were a fucking savage – maybe now you'll believe me. Look at me, I piss pure maiden's water.' And pointing himself over the side, he proved it.

'Oh Christ,' moaned Imeldo, half-weeping with incredulous relief, 'oh Christ, let me live like a saint and sin no more, not even the smallest, least enjoyable sin – but please, oh please, let me never suffer such a fright again.'

Epifanio was watching him, the glint of rough humour in his eye. 'Cheer up, at least you've learned something not many of us understand. You know now how a woman feels when she has her monthlies.'

Chapter Twenty-Three

THE NEXT DAY STARTED with an argument, but for once the fight was friendly, almost light-hearted. The date, they both agreed, was the 13th, but from that point their thinking pursued separate paths. Everyone knows, insisted Epifanio, that thirteen is an unlucky number, and desperate misfortunes most surely lay ahead of them. Rubbish, scoffed Imeldo, mere superstition; nothing could be worse than what they – and he most recently – had already been through. Had they bet upon the matter, however, Epifanio would have won hands down. Even many months later, both men were to acknowledge that the events of 13 January 1976 formed the very worst of their whole horrendous experience.

It was in the small hours of the morning, probably somewhere between two and three, that Imeldo, fitfully keeping watch, suddenly gasped, grabbed Epifanio's ankle, and shook it like a terrier with a bone.

'Wake up, your eyes are better than mine. For God's sake, Epifanio, wake up and tell me I'm not dreaming.'

Far away on the horizon, miles from where they lay, were the unmistakable lights of a large vessel; not just a distant glow but the sharp, defined and definable yellow glints of cabin portholes, row upon row of them.

'No, my God no, you're not dreaming.' Epifanio was near delirious with delight. 'That's a ship all right – a lovely, goddam ship.'

There followed the pantomime inseparable from such heart-stopping, emotionally-charged occasions. Unobserved in the darkness, they wept, they embraced, they shouted aloud and waved their arms wildly. Imeldo rummaged for the torch, found it and pointed it at the distant ship, but growled with disgust as the soaked batteries spilled out only a sickly gleam, barely visible across the breadth of the raft.

'I've seen more light,' swore Epifanio, 'in a whore's eyeball.'

Imeldo raked feverishly through the survival kit and finally brought out a flare. That, surely, would stand out against the blackness of the night and bring the ship steaming towards them. He took the cartridge by its handle, cursed as it slipped from his shaking fingers, and swore again as, retrieving it, he had to twist his head into a nearly impossible position in order to make out the instructions printed on the side. Because Imeldo, the patient, painstaking, thoughtful Imeldo had been guilty of one almost unbelievable oversight in his preparations for survival. Throughout all the long days they had passed, with time the only luxury in unlimited supply, not once had he made a detailed examination of the life-saving gear at their disposal. He therefore had not thought to keep the flares well protected in strips cut from the plastic sheeting. Worse, he had not even read and memorized the procedure for their operation. Had he done so, had he taken that surely most obvious of all precautions, he would have seen that the directions for holding and igniting the flares were based on the assumption that the user was right-handed – and Imeldo was left-handed.

His fingers were clumsy and the flare was damp. He had located the ignition fuse all right, but he was tugging blindly, pulling it uselessly in the wrong direction, and in sudden fury he hurled the thing from him, coming to his senses with a cry of shock only as he watched the first of their four such chances sink wasted into the sea. Fighting for control of his jumping, jangling, undisciplined nerves, he picked up another flare, not quite so wet as the first, and this time he handled it with more circumspection, enjoying one split second of triumph and relief as the fuse fizzed and started to sparkle. But once again, as he was left-handed, he was holding the flare the wrong way round, and he yelled in sudden agony as a stream of red-hot granules scorched across his knuckles and forced him to relinquish his grip. He howled yet again, this time in mental anguish, as the flare fell to the sopping floor and he watched helpless as it squandered its fire-power uselessly against the wet, dead bodies of the fish racked around the raft. He had time, even, to register that it incinerated not only their hopes, but also their larder. But the ship was still in sight, seemed even – or was he imagining things – to be drawing closer. Desperately he reached for the remaining flares, and he gave a quiet moan of utter, abject misery as his fingers pulled out two pulpy, sodden, worthless cylinders that lay like spoiled sausages in his palm. Close to breaking-point, he was only vaguely aware that Epifanio was shouting at him.

'Never mind the flares – you'll only set fire to the raft and us with it. We don't need them, Imeldo – can't you see? The lights are getting brighter. The Virgin has heard our prayers, and that ship's coming straight towards us.'

Imeldo strained his eyes along the line of Epifanio's outstretched, trembling arm, willing himself to believe, and yes, certainly, the lights of the ship were showing more clearly; they were going to be saved. But then he looked again, and turned reluctantly towards his companion with a sad, weary, defeated sigh. Imeldo was a sailor, and he could read the signals of the sea.

'You're right about the lights, Epifanio, they do look brighter, but only because our eyes are getting used to the dark. Look again, you'll see only two colours, and there should be three. Lots of yellow lights, and one or two red ones – even you know red means port. But we need green as well, green for starboard, and there's no green light there. She's moving all right, but she's moving across us, and that means she's moving away.'

The remaining hours of darkness neither man would choose to store among his memories. Both wept without shame, each desolate after his own fashion. Epifanio's bitter reproaches had been called down upon the Virgin, Imeldo's upon himself. Aware now of the full cost of his thoughtlessness, he was deeply ashamed, though not without a faint rebellious flicker of resentment. He had, after all, saved his companion and nursed him back to life. He had conscientiously and agonizingly kept double watch with red-raw, salt-caked eyelids that stung like scorpions. And he had dived and dived again to repair the raft even though he thought his lungs would burst. He had also used his skills and all but exhausted his patience in catching enough fish to feed them both. He had done all this with scarcely a word of complaint, but in a mere oversight, the sort of lapse anyone might suffer under stress, he had committed just one simple sin of omission. And for this single mistake he was being punished first by the sight and now by the memory of salvation sailing remorselessly away from them in an aureola of fading yellow light, a mocking caricature of the martyr's halo he had seen so often on the walls of the village church. For once wavering on the brink of blasphemy, he wondered if this was not a little less than fair, and it was in this brief moment of doubt that Imeldo's strong, life-preserving morale began to crumble.

Epifanio in the meantime, unable to rest despite the darkness, was talking of the visions that had been floating before his eyes, and he was unsure as to whether he had been awake or asleep.

'When I first saw that ship, Imeldo, I had this uncanny

feeling that I could reach out and touch it. My eyes knew it was miles away, but my heart and even my hands felt it was right there, close beside us. And then I saw myself at home, with my children all around me listening wide-eyed to the story of our adventure. All the village, young and old, had come out to greet us, you and me, with wine and tears and kisses. But then the picture began to fade, to dissolve the way it does in the movies, and I knew then that it just isn't going to be like that. You know it, too, don't you? We're never going to be rescued.

'What do you make of that deep down, Imeldo? Could God have been tantalizing us, holding out the promise of living and then snatching it away? Could He really be as cruel as that after all we've suffered already?'

He waited eagerly for some words of reassurance, but from Imeldo, for once, no comfort was forthcoming, and as Epifanio looked more closely at him, saw the staring eyes and the trembling, spasmodically jerking limbs, he felt the first stirrings of a fear so dreadful he would not allow it a name. For though Imeldo was shaking all over and his eyes were wild, he seemed possessed not so much by terror as by cold, pulsing anger. The knuckles showed white on his twisting fingers, he was chewing his lips till the blood ran. This was a man torn and driven by some terrible, deep-founded inner rage. Epifanio, half-hypnotised, sat watching him, and he, too, began to tremble.

'For God's sake, why won't you answer me?'

But Imeldo didn't answer, because the words would not come. His head was jerking up and down, from side to side, his cheeks mottled and suffused with blood, the veins in his throat knotted like cords in his efforts to speak, but the only sound to emerge was a strangulated moaning and a series of sub-human grunts. He was not at this moment a rational, thinking man. Though vaguely aware of Epifanio's voice, he heard it coming to him as if from the depths of the sea through a distorting rumble of mental confusion. He sensed only, with the horror of sudden awareness, that his mind was falling apart, and the one coherent message to form in his brain was a despairing, primeval urge to self-destruct. Epifanio, paralyzed by the visible disintegration of his former source of strength, watched motionless as Imeldo edged himself slowly, further and further, over the rim of the raft.

It may have been the cool touch of the water as it splashed in his face, or perhaps one final self-assertion of a deep-rooted will to live, but Imeldo himself, in the months ahead, was never able to feel certain of his motives at that moment of ultimate despair. Something, however, drew him back from the brink. It was not a complete change of heart; he experienced no sense of exultation or even of relief. It was, rather, an uncertain fumbling back towards reason, a dotard's dim awareness that his actions were still a matter of choice. And there was, too, something of the simpleton's sly cunning about what Imeldo did next.

Several times during the past two weeks, when his nerves had twanged too tautly over Epifanio's behaviour or when the heat of the midday sun had become unbearable, Imeldo had found relief in the rippling waters of the Pacific. With a bowline round his waist and the rope secured to a stanchion he had slipped over the side to cool himself both literally and metaphorically; one of man's oldest forms of therapy, it had never failed him. He decided to try it again now – with one small but vital change from the usual procedure. Waiting until Epifanio had retired once more to his plastic lair, he furtively, with the very minimum of movement, withdrew the surgical scissors from the survival kit and stowed them under the waistband of his trousers. No sound came from his companion, and Imeldo felt a half-crazy contentment; his options were still open, the choice was his, not God's. He would seek solace as usual in the lapping water. If it came, if this fever left his brain, then well and good – refreshed and returned to sanity, he would face another day. But if not, if the stroking movement of the water could no longer soothe him, if the torment and disorientation still raged in his mind, then he knew how to find the greatest peace of all. He would saw his way patiently through the slender manila rope and he would drift silently away, into eternity. Or, if the rope should prove too resistant to his slim little scissors . . . well, he could always use them on his wrists.

The splash of Imeldo's body tumbling over the side roused Epifanio from his torpor, and his first reaction was a shout of terror. He was convinced that his worst fears had been realized and that Imeldo, driven mad by disappointment, had decided to take his own life and leave his partner to drift on alone. Screaming the man's name, shuffling forward on his wounded legs, he reached out frantically over the rim of the raft, and it was only when he fell painfully over the 'suicide's' life-line that he saw Imeldo, safe and well, swimming along, keeping station with the raft. His pent-up fear exploded in a burst of fury.

'Imeldo, you bloody idiot, you scared the shit out of me – why in God's name couldn't you have warned me what you were going to do?'

Imeldo paid not the slightest attention, did not turn his head. Even in the broken blue of the water there remained an eerie, trance-like look about him, a fixed intensity in his unwavering stare as he continued to swim strongly, with almost lunatic determination, towards the distant shores of Japan. Epifanio sat back silently and left him in his madness.

For almost an hour Imeldo swam on and on, until at last he turned inwards and one thin and weary arm came reaching feebly over the wall of the raft. Epifanio watched warily, afraid of what he might see next, but at once came reassurance.

'Help me, I can't climb in by myself.'

Imeldo's voice, though weak, was clear and sane, and as Epifanio reached forward he saw that his eyes had lost their frenetic gleam. With powerful arms he helped the swimmer onboard, and a sense of relief flooded through him as Imeldo, after a few muttered words of thanks, rolled himself in the plastic sheeting and fell almost at once into a deep, calm and seemingly untroubled sleep. For the first time in the whole misadventure it was Imeldo who lay under protection and Epifanio who sat, pondered, and – almost without intention – kept watch. Not so much in the maritime sense, although he did now and again deign to scan the horizon, but rather as a sort of hospital vigil, warily alert for the first sign of returning madness. That was Epifanio's constant fear, that Imeldo, in his next bout of despondency, might again throw himself over the side, but this time without the rope.

Self-interest and street-wisdom set Epifanio to thinking and awoke in him, as conscience never could, an awareness that, whichever way they set the rules, this was a game for two players and the ball, beyond question, was now in his court. So far he had contributed nothing, had in fact repeatedly hindered Imeldo in his lonely efforts to keep the pair of them alive. That imbalance simply had to end – had in truth, he acknowledged, already ended.

Chapter Twenty-Four

EPIFANIO'S CHANGE OF ATTITUDE illustrated neither generosity of spirit nor any real sense of gratitude, but simply an unerring eye to the main chance. His native intelligence warned him that in slipping off into restful sleep Imeldo had shed not only his worries but also his responsibilities, and he could no longer be relied upon to fill the dual role of nursemaid and ship's master. Epifanio, therefore, must start to fend for himself.

But there was more to it, he realized, than that. Recalling the awful surge of fear he had felt when Imeldo plunged overboard, he knew with sudden certainty that alone on the raft he would not survive one single day; Imeldo, therefore, must also be looked after. That was Epifanio's newly acquired virtue – nobility born of self-interest – and it carried him through the rest of the night and well into the hours of daylight with scarcely one complaint or rough word to his companion. But in the early afternoon of the unlucky 13th, as Imeldo sat silently fishing to replenish the burned out larder, Epifanio awoke from his siesta with a bellow of anger.

'Stop that damned fish thrashing about – it's hurting my legs and keeping me awake.'

'Oh for God's sake, Epifanio, go back to sleep. You're dreaming, there's no fish in here and there won't be, either, if you don't shut up and give me a chance to catch some.'

'Well, something woke me up.' Epifanio was not to be appeased. He was still grumbling as he lay down again, but seconds later he was hauling himself upright and shouting.

'It's a ship, it's another bloody ship.'

Imeldo gazed eagerly around the horizon and then stared sourly at his shipmate. 'Still imagining things, are you – or was that meant to be funny? Get back to your bloody dreaming, Epifanio, there's not a damned thing in sight.'

'It doesn't have to be in sight.' Epifanio spoke in a whisper, hoarse from the wasted screaming of a few hours before. He lay down again on his side, his ear pressed to the thin floor of the raft. 'I can hear something, I tell you, and I swear to God it's the beat of an engine. Stand up – I can't – and look properly.'

Half hoping, half to humour him, Imeldo dragged himself to his feet and strained his eyes in a slow, systematic search all around him.

'Nothing, not a thing anywhere, and the light's perfect.'

'Maybe it is, but that's more than I can say for your eyes and ears.' Epifanio's words came in a throaty rasp of triumph as he raised his head from the sopping floor. 'Look again, and this time try keeping them open.'

Grudgingly, but impressed against his will by the confidence in Epifanio's voice, Imeldo once again hauled himself to his feet.

'Oh sweet Jesus, you're right, you're absolutely right. I can see her over there . . .' He pointed with a trembling finger. 'I see her right there, and, Epifanio, she's a big one.'

She certainly was a big one, possibly a passenger liner, but even a liner at such range looked little more than a splinter, and common sense should have warned them of the odds against their own tiny presence – a five-foot raft and two living skeletons – being detectable by eyes or by instruments over a distance of maybe seven or eight sea miles. But common sense had no chance against the desperation of men in such straits, and so there followed once again the grim charade of cheering, waving arms, the useless shouting and the tears of joy.

Joy that turned all too soon to misery, to a previously unknown depth of utter dejection as the big ship steamed steadily on her course, unaware of the two men dying within her easy reach. As she disappeared slowly over the horizon, Epifanio's words for once were spoken quietly and calmly, and for that very reason they had an ominous ring of truth.

'I tell you again, Imeldo, and this time I mean it from the bottom of my heart – I wish to God we'd both gone down with our mates. Admit it, we'd be a damn sight better off dead.'

Imeldo, beyond speech, offered no argument. Through all the remaining hours of daylight he uttered not one single word, but sat huddled, shoulders hunched, face buried in his hands, a silent study in total defeat. That night, for the very first time, he failed to keep watch, and when darkness fell he followed Epifanio's example, wrapped himself in the coverings, and lay on the floor of the raft with his eyes closed.

This time, however, the workings of his mind would not let him sleep. Was he perhaps, in God's eyes, as great a sinner as he himself considered Epifanio? Was this why the pair of them had been thrown together in such an unlikely way – as two wicked men marked for special torment? He had never thought of himself as wicked. Or – another and even more appalling possibility – did his own guilt lie in the very zeal and determination with which he had fought not only for his own life, but for Epifanio's? His whole being trembled at the thought; had he, Imeldo Barreto Léon, a humble seaman, been guilty of defying the will of the Lord God Almighty?

Imeldo moaned as he twisted and turned beneath his coverings, and the sheer horror of this last speculation gave birth to a solution to the problem, a solution as logical in its way as it was bizarre. He would put his life back into the hands of his Creator. The sighting of two major vessels within the space of a few hours showed that he and Epifanio were drifting into the busy lanes of Pacific shipping. Very well, let the Lord make clear His wishes and intentions. Henceforth Imeldo, like Epifanio, would keep no watch, day or night, but would simply lie with his eyes closed. They would drift, without knowing when it happened, into the path of the great liners, and perhaps one of these would either see them or sink them. If it came upon them in the night, if its grim iron bows simply sheared through their flimsy craft, tossing them into the sea, drowning them or crushing them as the huge bulk of the vessel thundered overhead – then so be it. It would all be over in minutes at the most; their agony would have ended, and the Lord would have had His way. But, if a ship should come across them in bright sunlight, and see them, and save them, and pull them aboard and welcome them with food, drink and warm blankets, then surely, because they had not striven to achieve it, this ending, equally, would represent God's will?

Well pleased with this lunatic logic, Imeldo felt better prepared to face whatever was left of the night and, perhaps, of his life – but he did not leave quite everything up to the Almighty. Once again he surreptitiously rifled the survival chest, and as he huddled down beneath the coverlet he clutched in his fingers a whole tube of the antiseptic and pain-killing tablets Epifanio had so stubbornly refused to take. The instructions for these he had, unlike the signal flares, studied closely, and he lay down secure in the knowledge that if God failed him and if life became more than he could endure, then he held the answer in his hand.

Chapter Twenty-Five

WHAT WAS LEFT OF THE DARKNESS passed without incident and next morning Imeldo, from force of habit, returned to his fishing. At first it was perfunctory, lacking all the zest and determination of earlier days, but a remarkable run of angler's luck – engineered, perhaps, by a whimsical Creator – restored his enthusiasm almost in spite of himself, and before long the spectre of starvation was once again in retreat. More than that, the entrapment and distribution of this new load of provender started a chain of action and reaction reflecting the changed relationship between the two survivors.

Epifanio, conscious of the demands likely to be made upon him in the days ahead – and perhaps reassured by the fact that Imeldo's recent blood-filled urine had clearly done him no harm – discovered for the first time that he could, after all, both swallow and hold down pieces of heart and liver from Imeldo's victims, and for once he lunched as heartily as his companion. Unfortunately, however, these tasty morsels nourished not only his body but also his bloody-mindedness, and very soon he was accusing Imeldo of keeping the most tempting specimens for himself. Imeldo's response was no less astonishing. Instead of telling Epifanio to go to hell, he began to use all his old fisherman's wiles – varying the bait, trawling the line shallow or deep, striking fast or letting the quarry run – in an effort to match each fish he caught with another one exactly like it, so that there could be no further charges of unfairness.

Epifanio would have none of it; with every hour that passed, with each titbit that was proffered, he grew steadily more aggressive and insulting. With his alley-fighter's instinct he knew exactly what he was doing, and it was not until many months later, when they were at last able to talk comfortably together, he discovered that his actions were based upon the same principle that his placid partner Imeldo, days before, had figured out for himself. In this late and desperate stage of their ordeal, the dominant character at any given moment would be better served by a companion who was angry and mentally active than by one who was passive, compliant, and consciously or subconsciously resigned to death. The reasoning was sound; just how sound neither man was to realize until much later.

For suicide, by now, had become for Imeldo a very real possibility and, more than that, almost an attractive one. His thoughts veered between religious dogma and upbringing on the one hand and sheer exhaustion of mind, body and spirit on the other. Held back from fatal action by the continuing conflict between fear of mortal sin and the aching, yearning desire to risk even damnation for the sake of rest, Imeldo in the event found at least a temporary answer not in the tenets of formal religion but in his own inborn decency, compassion and sense of responsibility. Responsibility, of course, to his wife and children; he had the wit to realize that a suicide bequeaths a legacy of guilt, however illogical and undeserved, to those he leaves behind. But he was equally aware of the more immediate consequences of self-destruction. He had already faced up to the fact that he could not survive without Epifanio, yet he was without doubt the morally stronger of the two; therefore, if he were to give up he would be betraying his weaker companion, condemning him also to death. This would be indefensible, a greater sin than suicide. This he could not and must not do.

And so, almost unintentionally and by different and devious routes, the two men had reached a situation in which the motivation of each acted to the benefit of both. Epifanio, determined to save himself, to that end would do his best also for Imeldo. Imeldo, rather than abandon Epifanio, would reluctantly take care of himself. Morally the two outlooks were poles apart, yet they combined to offer the greatest hope and prospect of survival. One quarrel, for example, at this very moment, led to unexpected events that brought both men boiling back to life.

Imeldo, having landed a few fish, was skinning, gutting and dissecting them, dropping the discarded scraps into a patch of plastic sheeting at his feet. The rising mound of bloody rubbish was not, admittedly, a pretty sight, and it aroused in Epifanio all his old feelings of revulsion – which he expressed in a picturesque stream of dockside imagery accompanied by a scatological survey of Imeldo's ancestry and character. Nerves were raw, tempers were short, and Imeldo, scooping up the offending offal in both hands, flung the steaming mass at the ranting, taunting face before him. His aim was wide, and the guts, bones and skin went sailing over the side. The two men, shame-faced but still breathing hard, relapsed into sullen silence, Imeldo picking up his hooks and line again in one last gesture of defiance.

This time, however, he had no success. He checked the spoon rig, changed the bait – still nothing. Puzzled, because of late the fish had been eager, almost queueing up to take the hook, he scanned the surface around the raft and for the first time in days found it undisturbed by so much as a splash or ripple; there was not one solitary Dory or Dorado in sight. He looked further afield, and his heart stopped dead. Down-current, where the discarded entrails had floated, the sea was being sliced into segments by a squadron of fast-moving dark triangles. Imeldo, after the first cold clutching of fear in his guts, glanced maliciously across to where his tormentor, unaware, was lying as usual with his eyes closed. This would give the bugger something to shout about. This would bloody teach him.

'Hey, Epifanio, don't look now, but we have company – right behind you.'

Epifanio raised his head and turned to gaze out over the side. His shout of terror might have summoned shipping.

'Sharks! Jesus Christ, Imeldo, sharks!'

'I didn't think they were goldfish. Well, now I know where our next meal has gone. They've more sense than to stick around with these fellows. Watch this . . .'

He picked up one of the empty water-cans, crammed it to overflowing with the scraps of fish still scattered around the floor, and heaved it into the sea. At once the foraging sharks broke formation and two dark shapes came zooming in like missiles, the first snatching the floating bait and swallowing it at a gulp. The other, since the food had completely disappeared, saw no cause to fight and rose, instead, to the surface, giving Imeldo his first good look at it.

'They're quite big ones, Epifanio – about ten feet long.'

'Quite big? – they're bloody monsters! What d'you think they'd do if one of us fell over the side?'

'Why – thinking of going for a swim? For Christ's sake, what do you think they'd do? We wouldn't make one decent meal for them between us.'

Epifanio, glowering, made no answer, and very soon he was, as usual, the first to bed down for the night. What did not match the established pattern was that he was also, on this occasion, the first to wake up.

Some hours after nightfall Imeldo, sleeping lightly, was disturbed by a faint rustling in the raft, and his eyes were open before he had made any other movement. As they became used to the darkness he saw first a hand and then a scrawny, oil-stained arm reach stealthily out from beneath the far corner of the plastic sheeting. Holding his breath, he watched as the hand crept like a spider, inching its way cautiously, silently across the floor until the fingers closed around the one object in the raft that was barred to them both, the tin of yellowed, dirty, brackish water that was their precious, pitiful, last protection against the day when their lives were finally running out. The fingers clutched, the arm moved backwards, Epifanio's head emerged from the coverings, mouth gaping wide, and the contents of the can vanished in one single greedy, untasting gulp. The tin was soundlessly replaced, the head and arm withdrew silently beneath the sheeting, and Imeldo, still motionless, uttered not one single word. He discovered to his own astonishment that he felt calm, almost rested, and was able to go quietly back to sleep when he ought, by all reason, to be screaming with rage. Even next morning his first comment, when it did come, was no more than a simple question, a genuine seeking for understanding.

'Tell me, Epifanio, why did you steal the last of our water when you know we've been keeping it for when it could save our lives?'

'Because I just couldn't stand it any longer – I get so thirsty.'

'And I don't – is that it?'

'I know, I know, and I'm sorry, Imeldo. But I just haven't got your willpower – you're a far stronger man than I am, and that's the plain truth of it.'

Imeldo sat looking at him, pondering over his words, and decided to let the matter rest.

Lethargy, in fact, overcame them both, for in their region of the Pacific the temperature that day reached 113° Fahrenheit, and an uneasy truce was observed as they idly poured cans of sea-water over each other to alleviate the scorching and shrivelling of their skin. From time to time Imeldo, keeping a sharp eye open for sharks, would slip over the side for a swim, but as the sun rose towards its zenith the accretion of salt encrusted like sharp gravel all over his body made the slightest brushing against the rough walls of the raft agony, and soon he was glad to lie still alongside Epifanio, with the plastic hood stretched over the four uprights to shield them from the worst of the direct heat. Even this small comfort had its price, for under the sagging roof the airless atmosphere seemed to press down as if smothering them with hot pillows, and for long hours neither man spoke nor cast so much as a glance towards the horizon.

Their day-dreams were shattered by a loud clattering and a bump that rocked the raft. Imeldo, peering out, saw an enormous black and white bird clinging precariously to one of the struts with its wide, webbed, scaly feet. Reacting fast he lunged forward, but the bird was too quick for him and, as it made its escape on ponderously beating wings, he sank back on his haunches with a disconsolate growl.

'Epifanio, were you awake for that? I just missed by a whisker the biggest duck I've ever seen.'

Even the landlubber was understandably sceptical. 'A duck? Out here?'

'Well it looked like a duck, or at least it had webbed feet – I saw them clearly, clinging to that post. No, maybe it was a bit big for a duck, and there was also something wrong about its beak. It turned down instead of up, and it was hooked, not flat – it looked sharp, too, and dangerous. Perhaps it's just as well I didn't get hold of it.'

Caution, however, was no match for curiosity and courage when the big bird came back half an hour later. This time, exhausted, it made no attempt to grasp a strut but simply thumped straight into the middle of the plastic canopy, bringing it down on top of the men underneath. With commendable presence of mind Imeldo held firmly to the leg he could feel pressing down on his chest, and with his other arm he reached blindly round the edge of the sheeting to grasp whatever should come to hand.

What came to hand was a thick, powerful throat, twisting and turning in a frenzy of fear. Taking a chance, Imeldo let go his clumsy grip on the creature's leg and applied all his strength to the main point of attack. Squeezing until his arms ached, ducking and dodging to evade the slashing and the pecking as the hooked, ugly bill of the albatross sliced back and forth, from side to side, within inches of his unprotected eyes, he dug his fingers and thumbs deeper and deeper into the feathered, muscular flesh and at last, when he felt he could hold on no longer, he won. The 'big duck' suddenly quivered, writhed, reared its head, and vomited its latest and still undigested catch – two squid hot from their intestinal incarceration and four small fishes still smelling freshly of the sea. To complete the surrender the bird gave one feeble beat of its great wings and flopped dismally to the floor, so docile that the two men were able without risk to tether it by its legs in one corner of the raft, where for the next hour it pecked and fretted at its bindings but made no serious effort to escape.

Imeldo, sniffing over the bird's offerings and finding them good, was in better spirits than he had been for days.

'My God, but we're in luck. We'll soon have our first decent meal since the *Istra*. Squid needs no cooking at all – we always used to catch it and eat it when we were out after tuna. It's beautiful, sweet as a nut, and more than that, it'll quench your thirst. Here – have one.'

As he talked he dangled the two squid over the side, rinsing away any signs or flavour of the albatross' inner workings, and he handed one over to Epifanio with a cheerful grin. A death's-head image stared back at him, and the response came in a horrified, incredulous croak.

'You're going to eat *that* – a fucking octopus that's been stewing inside a sea-bird's guts? I don't believe it, I just don't bloody believe it, Imeldo, not even of you. Come on man, please – tell me you're joking.'

'Like hell I'm joking. Listen, Epifanio, every kid who ever fished around our islands has eaten squid and loved it. Just think of the shops at home, and the cafés and restaurants. Squid's a delicacy, and even the tourists pay big money every day to eat it served in its own ink.'

'I don't give a shit for the tourists, or for you either. I've never eaten slimy squid, raw or cooked, and I'm damned if I'm going to start now.'

Imeldo sat back with an airy wave of his unoccupied hand. 'Suit yourself, I'll have them both.' He hesitated, hoping that Epifanio's refusal had stemmed from instinct rather than conviction.

'Think, Epifanio, think of all the bars at home you've ever been in. That's quite a few – and in every single one of them, admit it now, you've seen men just like us at the *tapas* counter paying good money for exactly what's in front of you now, except that theirs isn't so freshly caught.'

He paused, looking keenly at his companion to see if he had made any impression, but found to his irritation that Epifanio was not listening to him at all. Instead he was gazing at the albatross with a vague, dreamy look in his eyes that Imeldo had never seen before, and at that very moment, quite casually, he reached out his hand, offering it a morsel of fish. The murderous looking bill slashed out at him, but quite unconcerned he withdrew his hand calmly and continued to stare at the bird with unruffled composure. Then, turning slowly, he spoke to Imeldo in a voice completely unlike his own, not a grousing rasp, not a querulous whine, but a gentle voice, a voice that might have come wafting on the breeze from the hills of Assisi.

'Let this poor creature go, Imeldo. It has done us no harm. Why should we treat it like an enemy?'

Imeldo stared terrified at this stranger, and so there began another brief chapter in their saga.

Chapter Twenty-Six

HERE WAS SOMETHING new and unknown: Epifanio the mystic, Epifanio cast ludicrously out of character as St Francis. Imeldo eyed him carefully, the man didn't sound quite sane.

'This creature lives on fish, Imeldo, yet it refuses fish. It's weak and must be starving, but it snaps at me when I try to feed it. It must be even more frightened than hungry.'

'More bloody angry, I should think, after being half-throttled and tied to a post. And its belly was full enough five minutes ago, if you remember, with food to feed it – or us – for days. It may be tired, but it's not dying, and if I were you I'd keep my hands to myself – one good nip with that beak could have your fingers off.'

But Epifanio was far away, wistful, in a dream world of his own.

'If only we had paper and a pencil, this bird could save us. We'd set it free with a message tied to its leg, a message reading: "On a raft in the Pacific Ocean there are two survivors from the *Berge Istra*, sunk on 30 December 1975." We'd sign it with our names, and the bird would carry it back to land and the world and our families would know we were safe.'

'Sure, sure – and if only we had a short-wave radio we could send out a distress signal and save the poor bloody bird all that trouble. For God's sake, Epifanio, stop drivelling. This damn duck's going to save us all right, but not by carrying imaginary messages written on paper we don't have with a pencil that doesn't exist. It's going to save us because it's going to feed us after we've slit its throat. A nice bit of duckling'll make a change from fish, and there should be enough blood in it to keep our mouths moistened for days.'

'Don't kill it. Set it loose and let it fly away to freedom. Something tells me that this should be its destiny – and ours.'

'And something tells me that you've slipped your moorings. What's the matter with you – don't you want to live? We can eat now, and we can drink, and all we have to do is wait for someone to pick us up. And we'll soon be in amongst the Japanese fishing fleet.'

What Imeldo said was logical, and it was also true; their chance of rescue was better now than it had ever been, provided they kept themselves alive. The flesh and blood of the albatross would make that not only possible but almost certain, so long as Epifanio did not finally succumb to the creeping poison in his legs, which were now visibly rotting away.

And yet, for reasons that neither then nor later was Imeldo able to explain, he found himself gradually but assuredly losing the debate – for it never became a real argument, still less a quarrel. There was something almost hypnotic, it seemed, about Epifanio's impassioned pleading; the tears coursed down his cheeks as he begged that the creature's life should be spared. And to this, incredibly, Imeldo eventually agreed, knowing that he might pay for his submission with his life. With no more than a sigh of resignation he untied the ropes holding the albatross to the strut, and he lifted the bird, now docile, over the rim of the raft and settled it gently on the water. For several minutes it lay at rest, scarcely stirring, and then, with a busy fluttering that grew to a steady, powerful beat, it spread its great wings and soared, circling the raft several times as if in valediction before slowly disappearing into the distance and from their sight.

As Epifanio gazed after it, a benign smile on his weatherbeaten face, Imeldo began to think deeply about the phenomenon he had just witnessed, the extraordinary volte-face which had transformed a brutal, harsh, and totally selfish man, an experienced and enthusiastic hunter with gun and trap who for years had fed his family on partridge and rabbit from the hills of Taganana, into a soft-hearted humanist who valued the freedom of an albatross above its life-saving quality as a source of food. Nothing about the experience seemed to make sense. A hunter of game who refused to kill; a man who had learned to swallow the raw liver of a fish, but turned his nose up at breast of 'duck'; a coward so afraid of death that he saw poison in a penicillin pill or injection, but who now gave away enough food to keep him safe from starvation for many days to come; a man low enough to steal a comrade's last sip of water, now crying his eyes out over the safety of a bird. Truly, mused Imeldo, this Epifanio is a strange and complex man, a seething mass of contradictions, and with this thought he began to speak, edging himself carefully closer and closer towards the sensitive, dangerous subject now uppermost in his mind.

'Y'know, you're a funny fellow, Epifanio. After fighting for days against the notion of raw fish, you find you can eat it – but then you go all squeamish about squid, which guys like us have been eating raw all our lives. And now you've made me – oh yes, I know I agreed to it, but you made me agree with your persuasion and your pleading – you've made me throw away a bloody banquet. Now I'm not complaining, but I want you to tell me just one thing – why?'

'I don't know, honestly I don't. I just felt so sorry for it.'

'I believe you. Well I have to, I mean I saw you and listened to you, but it's still got me beat. When you're out shooting rabbits you don't start weeping over dear little fluffy bunnies

– you skin the buggers and put them in the pot – so what was so special about that bloody duck?'

Epifanio looked at him long and thoughtfully, as if debating whether to reply. And then, almost counting his words . . .

'That's just it. Look, I don't know how to say this, and God knows I certainly can't explain it, but there did seem to be something special about it. I had this queer feeling inside me that we were being told to set it free, that it would be almost sacrilege to kill it. You can laugh, but something seemed to be saying that if we killed that creature we'd receive a far greater punishment than anything we've suffered so far.'

Imeldo had seldom felt less like laughing. Gingerly, in real fear of what reaction his words might bring, he led the conversation towards the vital question.

'Well I don't think God can punish us much more than He has already, and I can't honestly see why He should want to, with or without a sea-bird in our stomachs. But Epifanio, this is what really puzzles me – why should you feel so badly over taking the life of a bird, any bird, when you've already murdered a human being?'

'When I've *what*? Are you crazy?'

'Come on, Epifanio, we all knew about it, everyone on the ship. Manuel Linares was a good friend of mine, but I wasn't the only one he talked to about why he was quitting. "Watch out for the man from Taganana,", that's what he said before he went ashore at Las Palmas. "Keep well clear of him, because he's served nine years for murder." Manuel was no coward, I know that for sure, but he was frightened enough of you to throw up his job. So I'm asking you again, Epifanio – what makes a murderer give a shit about a sea-bird?'

The tension suddenly seemed almost tangible and Imeldo, watching warily, wondered for a moment if he would come under attack. Epifanio's expression was hidden from him because his head was down, waving slowly from side to side. Whether in disbelief or in denial Imeldo was unsure, but the shaking shoulders betrayed the strength of his emotions. Epifanio buried his face in his hands, his lean brown fingers squeezing and flexing as if to knead some comfort into the flesh and the troubled spirit beyond it. He strove manfully to still the quivering of his upper body, and only then looked up – that was when the outraged Imeldo discovered that the emotion overcoming Epifanio was not anger, but helpless, uncontrollable mirth.

'Me a convicted murderer? For God's sake use the brains you were born with. When I came to sea I was thirty years old, and I already had seven kids. How the hell d'you think I sired them from my cell – by remote control? And since when did Sig. Bergesen make a habit of hiring murderers? Look, Imeldo, I've been a hard man in my time and I have a rough tongue when I choose to use it – but I don't go around killing people.'

'But Linares . . . he said you told him all this yourself, and he certainly believed it or he'd never have left the ship.'

Epifanio gave a crooked, almost pitying smile. 'Sure I told him all that, and the dumb bugger believed me. Sorry – I forgot he was a friend of yours, but he was a dumb bugger to take in such a tale, and he was no friend of mine. If you want to know, I was a bit slow and clumsy in picking up what he was teaching me about tying knots, and he started calling me names and giving me a hard time. So I gave him a mean look and a tall story, just a sort of warning to get him off my back – him and some of the others who'd been riding me. I've never given it another thought to this day. How was I to guess he'd take it so seriously? I mean, I ask you, does our government go handing out passports and foreign shipping documents to guys they've sent to jail for murder?'

Imeldo winced, uncomfortably aware that Epifanio's derision could with equal logic be directed at himself, but he came back gamely enough in an effort to save face.

'No need to be so cocky about it. Maybe Linares wasn't as dumb as all that – every man in the crew believed that story, and that should tell you something.'

'Tell me what?'

'Tell you you were such a nasty bit of work that thirty men and women who lived with you, saw you every day, were quite ready to believe you'd done time as a killer. And d'you know what? It shocked us a bit when we heard it, but it didn't really surprise us. That's not the sort of impression I'd like to have made on the folk I work with.'

Epifanio was no longer laughing. He seemed, instead, on the brink of tears.

'Are you serious, Imeldo? Did everyone really think as badly of me as all that?'

Still smouldering with resentment over the deception that had cost him so much in unnecessary fear, Imeldo for once was brutal.

'Of course we did. Why d'you think men avoided you on the ship – because you couldn't tie knots? Don't be bloody stupid. Why d'you imagine I threw away the finest tool we had, the clasp-knife? Because I was afraid I'd wake up one night with it sticking in my guts. And I'll tell you something else, that damned silly story of yours very nearly cost you your life. Because you can take my word for it, Epifanio – when I saw who it was I'd dragged out of the sea, I came close as a whisker to shoving you right back in again.'

Epifanio's smile was twisted and ugly. 'That would've made you the murderer, wouldn't it? Yet you sit there calmly telling me you thought about it – maybe you're not such a fucking saint yourself, now are you?'

'No, I'm not. But I didn't ditch you, even though it scared me shitless just knowing you were lying next to me. No, instead of pushing you back over the side I sucked all that stinking garbage from your guts. I'm no bloody saint, as you say – but I saved your life.'

In all his forty years no words had ever hit Imeldo with the paralyzing force of Epifanio's cool, sardonic rejoinder:

'Well, I guess that makes us even, doesn't it?'

It seemed like hours before Imeldo recovered sufficiently to speak, and when he did it was in a confused, incredulous whisper.

'Just what, in God's name, are you talking about? What in hell have you ever done for me?'

The lop-sided, cynical grin had returned to Epifanio's face, and he looked at Imeldo curiously, almost wonderingly. 'You really don't know, do you? Tell me, my hero, how did you get clear of the *Istra* in the first place? And how did you come to be still living after all the others went down?'

'You know perfectly well. I was blown overboard in the last explosion, and then I found this raft.'

'So you did, so you did, and you very kindly pulled me in alongside you. But how did this raft happen to float free when the others were still tied to the ship?'

'Because I'd unlashed it, that's why. Imeldo made no attempt to disguise his mounting irritation, but was vaguely troubled to notice once again a gleam of sour amusement in Epifanio's steady gaze.

'That was clever of you – really quick-thinking. Whatever put it into your mind in all that noise and confusion?'

'Well if you must know, it was someone else's idea. I was going for the boats, and he . . .'

Imeldo faltered, and his eyes grew round and disbelieving as he stared at his companion. Epifanio stared straight back at him.

'That's right. You were so fucking shocked, you didn't even see the man who pulled you back. Maybe now you know why I reckon we're all square.'

Chapter Twenty-Seven

'But why didn't you tell me? Why've you never said anything about this before? I just can't understand you. We've argued, we've quarrelled, I've called you all the names on this earth, and meant it – how could you, of all men, manage to keep your mouth shut? And why?'

Epifanio, more relaxed than Imeldo had ever seen him, answered easily, as if enjoying some very special inner satisfaction.

'You're right, you can't understand me, you'll never understand me or anyone like me. Listen, Imeldo, I'm as much a hunter on the streets and in the bars as ever I was in the hills of Taganana, and I've learned a bit. I know when I've got a good card or a good weapon in my hand, and I save it for when it'll be most use.' He gave a little chuckle, and there was a good-humoured glint in his eye. 'And it shut you up pretty sharply, didn't it? Maybe now you'll ease up a bit on the Sunday school lectures.'

Imeldo, crestfallen but grinning at his own discomfort, would have been hard pushed for a reply, but he was spared the necessity as Epifanio, dragging himself upright, pointed out across the ocean and, laughing hysterically, began to shout at the top of his voice.

'Look over there, Imeldo. It's land – I can see land.'

Across the horizon, far away to one side of them, both men could dimly make out the misty blue hills and hollows of an island, a large, long island. Without hesitation they went to work. Imeldo seized a rigid hatch-cover and began to paddle furiously across the easterly current, while his companion for once showed willing by picking up an empty water can and starting to bail the dregs of sea-water from the slopping floor.

It was late afternoon when they began, and in the heat of the sun the labour seemed endless, but they roused each other to greater efforts with shouted reports that they were making progress, easily verified by the changing shape of their destination.

'How much longer, Imeldo?'

'Who cares? I can see tall trees now – just you keep bailing, and I'll keep paddling.'

The sun was going down when Epifanio spoke next, his voice small and tremulous like a child's in the dark.

'Imeldo, the trees look different now. They're not so tall any more, but they're bigger and fatter.'

'Nonsense, it's only the sunset and shadows and sea mist. Don't lose heart – we're getting there.'

For a little while longer they ploughed on steadily at their chosen tasks, and then . . .

'Don't bother paddling any more, Imeldo – and don't bother to argue. Just look over there, our island's vanishing.'

Ahead of them a long, low, dark cloud reflected the last of the evening sunshine like a huge dead fish floating belly-up on the surface of a sparkling, pearl-grey sea. And Imeldo, in a flat voice said quietly, without raging or tears, 'I think, my friend, we have just enjoyed what travellers call a mirage.'

He sat there utterly dispirited, staring out at the shifting configuration of the 'island' while Epifanio, without a word, rolled himself in his coverings and lay down on the floor as if he might never again even bother to wake up.

Sleep would not come, though, to Imeldo, and to take his mind off his misery he turned, as always, to his fishing tackle.

In the twilight he sat hunched over the rim of the raft, scarcely caring whether he attracted a catch but soothed and pacified by the gentle dragging of the lure on his line. His eyelids at last began to droop, and he was dozing when, with a jolt like a railcar hitting a siding, he toppled forward and very nearly over the side. He caught a glimpse of the silver spoon rig diving steeply towards the depths, and seconds later the pull was repeated, more powerfully even than before. Whatever he had hooked began now to fight desperately for its life and freedom, and with all his strength and skill he had to play the fish, to keep it moving yet under control, to ease it gradually towards him, although always ready to anticipate the sudden movement that would snap the line like a thread and rob him for ever of his precious hooks and lures. His arms ached fiercely and he thought of calling on Epifanio for help, but then he thought, no – fishing and Epifanio just didn't go together and, anyway, it would be brutal to ruin the man's temporary escape into sleep. But the weight on his muscles was enormous, and for one mad second a sickening image flickered across his mind – had he struck into the long-lost body of some sailor more luckless than himself?

Angrily he pulled himself together. Rubbish; dead sailors don't jump around jerking live sailors into the sea. But his nerve had been shaken, and he was almost glad of the agonizing distraction as once again the nylon line ran humming and sizzling across his palm and he saw the blood shoot out in little fountains from his red-raw, tortured fingers. He had been battling with this invisible adversary for the better part of an hour when, from his fisherman's instinct and long years of experience, he sensed rather than felt that the fight had gone out of it. Blowing on his lacerated hands, for the first time fully conscious of the pain, he began to draw the creature slowly, and with infinite care, closer and closer to the raft, and as it broke the surface with its ugly snout he thanked the good Lord that he'd had the wit not to waken Epifanio.

It was not very big, admittedly, as sharks go, but at five feet it was almost as long as Imeldo himself, and with its multiple rows of serrated teeth it was infinitely better armed. Imeldo, in truth, will go to his grave still wondering what lunacy persuaded him, having seen this lethal monster, to spend another hour letting it exhaust itself completely, before hoisting it over the gun'le, still alive and feebly snapping, into the cramped and shabby habitat shared by Epifanio and himself.

Yet that was what he did, this slender fisherman from Tenerife, and in his heart he knows why. It was a challenge no true angler could resist. With the shark flailing wildly, and with a stark-eyed Epifanio shouting blue murder as he cowered in the furthest cranny of the raft, Imeldo grabbed the hatchcover, the one he had used as a paddle, and having beaten his opponent into stunned submission, jammed it between its jaws, locking them wide open. He then sat gazing with satisfaction at as fine a trophy as any fisherman, anywhere any time, could hope to claim honourably as his own.

On shore, however, those concerned with the fate of the *Berge Istra* had no cause for celebration, and on 16 January the reports in Britain's national newspapers were gloomy. The words of the *Daily Telegraph* spoke for them all:

US PLANES DROP SEARCH FOR SHIP

'*United States Air Force aircraft seeking the missing Norwegian ore carrier* Berge Istra *temporarily abandoned the search yesterday after unsuccessfully sweeping an area of the West Pacific. If the* Berge Istra *has sunk, it will be one of the largest individual merchant ship losses in maritime history. The vessel itself is valued at more than 18 million dollars.'*

Had the contents of this bulletin been known to the occupants of the raft it is doubtful whether, at this time, the message would have affected them greatly one way or the other. Both were now very conscious of approaching death, and neither really cared. Epifanio's mind, once filled with terror at the very thought of it, now simply rejected it, and allowed him to pass most of his hours in oblivion. Imeldo had started once again, and more positively, to welcome the concept, seeing death as a release, and a passport to heaven, for his religious convictions were still very strong. Not strong enough, though, should release be too long delayed, to dismiss altogether the idea of self-destruction, and it was this that most constantly occupied his thoughts as he sat with his line at the rim of the raft.

His responsibility to Epifanio, for example; he now saw that differently, yet could not feel absolved from it. Previously he had acknowledged that he must force himself to survive because he was the stronger of the two. Now, as he felt his hopes, his courage, and his resolution crumbling away to nothing inside him, he no longer considered this so. Epifanio's innate toughness and his street-cunning might well outweigh his own high-minded morality – but even as he flinched shame-faced at this thought, another and even more disturbing possibility rose up before him to take its place.

What if Epifanio's self-constructed reputation had spread beyond the confines of the *Berge Istra* to the relatives of her crew and throughout the districts of Tenerife where most of them lived? Supposing Imeldo were to die by his own hand and Epifanio, by some chance, were to survive? Just how hard might Epifanio then find it to convince relatives and friends that Imeldo was indeed a suicide? His religious convictions were well-known, his love for his family almost a local legend; who would believe that with rescue at hand this man had wilfully killed himself, leaving his wife and his children to suffer and grieve?

My God, thought Imeldo, if I were to throw myself overboard, leaving Epifanio to survive, I might be branding him for ever as a murderer, for he wouldn't be able to laugh this story to scorn as he did the other.

Imeldo was about to slip over the side, not to end things but to swim, to reflect on this sombre thought, and to bring cool reason to his fevered brain when, suddenly, with a roaring like an express train rumbling through a tunnel, the sea all around him became a swirling maelstrom of foam and confusion, and a school of dolphins, leaping and snorting with delight, began to circle the raft. A reminder, mused the chastened Imeldo, that the world was still full of life and beauty, and for that day, at least, he put all thoughts of self-destruction firmly from his mind.

Chapter Twenty-Eight

NEXT MORNING BEGAN with the matter of the shark. A fine specimen and a magnificent capture it might be, but even Imeldo could scarcely dispute Epifanio's disgruntled objection that the brute took up space in the tiny raft out of all proportion to its nutritional value, and apart from that, unless it was gutted, it would start to smell after a few hours under the broiling sun.

And so Imeldo reluctantly reached for the scissors and began the long task of cutting the corpse to pieces. He was determined that some benefit should derive from the titanic struggle that had cost him not only effort beyond measure but also the skin from his hands. He set aside as usual the heart and the liver and then, as he scissored away at the main body of the fish, he gave Epifanio a little lecture intended not only to inform, but also to justify the importance he himself had attached to catching and landing such a monster in the first place.

'I've often heard,' he began, sententiously and quite untruthfully, 'that if you scatter the pieces of a dead shark over the water, it will serve as a sort of warning and keep the other sharks away. So this one will be useful, if only in allowing me to swim in peace.' With this he continued to slice busily and later, with due ceremony, he cast out his home-made shark-repellent in handfuls that drifted sluggishly away without any visible effect on marine life in the area.

This face-saving activity did, however, achieve something

of value, for in the course of it Imeldo came upon a new and desperately needed source of drinkable liquid, albeit in minuscule measures. While reaching over the side with the scraps of shark meat he caught sight of several clusters of rough excrescences on the underside of the raft, and with the scissors he scraped in a few handfuls for a closer look. Which was how he discovered that barnacles in sufficient quantity could provide a welcome and thirst-quenching addition to their diet.

Another discovery that day, made by Imeldo on waking from an afternoon siesta, was at first more mysterious and later, infinitely less agreeable. While asleep he had found himself, for the first time, dreaming that he was back on the *Berge Istra*, and not during the horrendous moments of her destruction. He could see the men working around him, he could hear the sounds of the engine-room, he could smell the pungent odour of the oil. This last hallucination had been the most powerful of all, because as he struggled back to wakefulness he could still smell it. Only then, opening his eyes wide, did he realize that as they both slept they had drifted into the middle of a huge, endless slick of oil – a heart-breaking discovery that suggested only one terrible, unthinkable circumstance. Gazing frantically all around him, Imeldo ruthlessly kicked Epifanio, yelling at him to rouse himself and join in the search.

'Oh Jesus, I can't believe it. Now tell me I was wrong about keeping a constant watch. My God, don't you see what's happened?'

An ill-tempered Epifanio scarcely raised his head from the floor. 'No, I'm damned if I do, and I don't care. What's wrong with you this time – caught another shark, or is it a whale maybe?'

The fury rising suddenly in Imeldo's throat died just as quickly into bleak, toneless despair. 'Never mind – go back to sleep. We've just missed another ship, that's all, a ship discharging oil right alongside us – and we both slept right through it. I tell you, Epifanio, we don't bloody well deserve to be saved.'

'I don't give a damn whether we're saved or not, so don't give me any more of your crap about watches and signals. Listen, Imeldo, if a ship comes heading right towards us, and you can hear them shouting, and smell hot sweet coffee – then give me a shout. Until then, just leave me alone.'

Imeldo was happy to take him at his word, and the two men exchanged not another word before nightfall. Meanwhile, long before dusk on that same day, 17 January 1976, the Rescue Co-ordination Center at Kadena Air Force Base issued the following statement: 'The United States Air Force in Okinawa has suspended indefinitely the search for the *Berge Istra*.'

Imeldo and Epifanio, of course, knew nothing of this official abandonment of hope, which was more or less coincidental with their own, and for them 18 January began as just another day. Epifanio slept as usual, whilst Imeldo fished, occasionally catching a Dory or a Gallo, despite the sea's filmy covering of oil. It was mid-morning before anything untoward happened to break the dreary, familiar pattern of the past three weeks. Imeldo, rummaging idly through the remnants of gear thrown casually together in the emergency hatch, came across at the bottom of the heap a flare that had somehow been overlooked. Since now there was no urgency he took the trouble this time to examine it more closely than he had its wasted predecessors, and out of curiosity he unwound a threaded attachment he found at one end. This exposed a black, waxy substance, while the inside of the screw-cap, he noticed, formed an abrasive strip. Without thinking, he rubbed the two surfaces briskly together, just as if striking a match.

Which was, of course, exactly what he was doing. He jumped in sudden fright as the sparks flew up towards his face and flung the rocket away from him, into the sea, where it fizzed and sparkled and, floating as it was designed to float, began pouring into the empty air a great towering pillar of orange-coloured smoke.

Imeldo, appalled at this criminal waste, looked fearfully at the far corner and sighed with heart-felt relief as Epifanio snored on beneath his blanket. But long afterwards, as they drifted on, he could still see the orange cloud floating in the sky, and he was watching it wistfully, sad rather than angry at his own foolishness, when out from his coverings came Epifanio, bellowing like a bull.

'This is it, Imeldo – this time it's really it. There's a ship out there – I heard it quite clearly – and this time it's coming our way.'

But Imeldo could not bring himself to look, could not bear the thought of another disappointment more bitter even than the last, a disappointment that would surely drive him senseless with guilt over the wasted flare, and so he sat still as a stone. Epifanio meanwhile, staring at Imeldo with undisguised scorn, somehow forced himself up on to his wounded knees and clung fiercely to the nearest strut. His hunter's eyes were as keen as his hunter's ears were sensitive.

'It's a ship all right – I can see it now, clear as bloody crystal, and it's heading straight towards us.'

Imeldo, struggling to his feet, found his legs were like jelly and would not support him, and he slumped back to the floor like a discarded puppet. But only for seconds. Then he was up again, standing over Epifanio, one arm round his shoulders, the other joining in the crazy semaphore as they shouted, screamed and waved madly with anything that came to hand.

At last, even for Imeldo, there could be no doubt, no doubt at all. They could see the ship plainly, a fishing-boat, and they could see the men aboard her handling ropes and tackle, making ready to pick them up.

'Virgin of the Snows,' breathed Epifanio, 'I promise you six hundred *pesetas*, and another six hundred to the Virgin of Begona. What promise are you making, Imeldo?'

Imeldo's eyes were misted. 'I vow, Epifanio, that for the rest of my life I will walk bare-footed each year in the procession behind the image of St Matthew, the patron saint of Punta de Hidalgo.'

Wide-eyed they watched the approach of salvation, and within minutes they could make out the name of their rescuer, the fishing-boat *Hachi-Ho-Maru No. 6*. Then came the greatest moment of their lives. Japanese faces were grinning down at them, hands were stretched out to greet them and to steady them, ropes and grapples came snaking down to secure the broken, bedraggled plastic platform that had been their home these past three weeks. A steel ladder was slung from the trawler's hand-rail, and so low was she in the water that Imeldo was able to climb stiffly, shakily aboard her with no help beyond a few welcoming hands to grasp and to support his arms.

With tears streaming down his face he embraced the first of his rescuers as two other members of the crew shinned swiftly down the ladder to lift and carry Epifanio to safety. The Japanese skipper, beaming, came down from the bridge, shook hands with the pair of them and, pointing to the raft, enquired with gestures and raised eyebrows whether he should salvage it or cut it adrift. Their answer was never in doubt; they had hated that raft, God knows, for what seemed as long as they could remember, but that same shabby platform had saved them, and it represented to each of them something deeper than the most eloquent words could have expressed. The skipper, reading their eyes with perfect understanding, gave his orders, and moments later the raft and its rag-bag of contents and equipment was hoisted on board and lashed to the trawler's deck.

At the centre of things, however, activity was less disciplined. Imeldo could not stop himself from shouting, weeping, jumping up and down. Epifanio, less mobile but equally uninhibited, expressed his emotions by crawling round in circles on the deck, grinning and yelping like a mongrel pup. The Japanese crewmen crowded round them, smiling and cheering and offering them milk and coffee, bread and jam, even bars of soap and rough face-cloths. The first few sips of hot liquid set the two survivors trembling and then caused them to double over, clutching their stomachs in an agony of cramp, but wrapped in blankets they recovered rapidly, so much so that Imeldo had a second of inspiration. Up to this point only signs and gestures had conveyed anything to either side; not one spoken term had been intelligible. Now Imeldo reached into the raft and, pulling aside a tattered strip of the weather-hood, pointed melodramatically to the printed legend thus revealed; stencilled in bold block letters along the side wall were the two words recognizable to any ship's captain on the Pacific Ocean – *Berge Istra*. The reaction was like the blue-paper lighting of an Oriental crackerjack. The first man to see the name shouted wildly to the mate, the mate relayed the news to the captain, the captain took a look for himself to make quite sure and rushed to the radio. The world was about to learn the fate of the *Berge Istra*.

The contents of that first brief signal, sent in understandable haste by the Japanese skipper before he had even thought to discover the survivors' names, told more than a detailed description ever could about their physical condition at the moment of rescue. 'From the ore carrier *Berge Istra*, which had sunk after three explosions,' he had picked up, he now reported, 'two survivors, one white and one black.'

This misunderstanding about the ethnic origin of the two men resulted not from the filth that coated them – Epifanio, who had floated in oil at the time of the sinking, was in fact the one regarded by his rescuers as white – but from sunburn, and it was Imeldo who, after his countless hours of fishing and wakefulness, was no longer recognizable as a white European. It had been, beyond question, a close-run thing, and doctors were later to give the opinion that neither man was likely to have survived more than another twenty-four hours of dehydration and exposure.

But now they were in the safe hands of the captain and crew of the *Hachi-Ho-Maru No. 6*. Epifanio's hideously wounded legs and back were bathed and treated with soothing ointment by the skipper himself, while Japanese seamen vied with each other in providing cigarettes, sweets, fresh drinks and clean linen. Slowly, armed with paper and pencils they also elicited Imeldo's and Epifanio's names, their relatives' names, their places of origin, and at least the bare bones of their adventure and of the fate that had befallen their comrades and their ship.

On 18 January, just one day after the United States Air Force had ended its massive air-sea rescue operation over the Pacific, the United States Coast Guard was able to issue the first official report of the rescue. By the following day the captain of *Hachi-Ho-Maru No. 6* had issued further reports and Reuters, United Press International and other news agencies across the world were adding further details about the movements of the two central characters and their rescuers as they gradually emerged.

These movements proved maddeningly slow and frustrating

not only to Imeldo and Epifanio, but also to the representatives of the world's media who had converged upon the islands of the Pacific with their notepads, cameras and teleprinters, eager to interview the heroes of the greatest maritime mystery story in years.

For the *Hachi-Ho-Maru No. 6* was a fishing vessel at the start of her voyage and her admirably professional captain, whilst delighted to rescue two sailors in distress and to offer them every comfort, had not the slightest intention of returning to his home port – and his employers – with an empty hold. And so for the next three days, as the trawler cast her nets and landed her catch, Imeldo and Epifanio had no option but to control their impatience and show civility and proper gratitude to those who had, after all, just saved their lives.

Chapter Twenty-Nine

FEELINGS OF GRATITUDE CAME readily enough, even to Epifanio, for they were treated like royalty. Certain aspects of Japanese hospitality, however, did briefly pose problems. At the first proper meal the knobbly nuggets of cauliflower, fried in batter and served on a bed of fluffy, snow-white rice, both looked and smelled enticing – but the savoury aroma was the only gastronomic treat they could enjoy, for neither man had the slightest notion how to pick up grains of rice with a pair of chopsticks. Inbred Spanish courtesy restrained them – just – from shovelling in the tempting food with their fingers, and fortunately the difficulty was swiftly resolved when one of their hosts ran giggling to the galley and returned with forks and spoons.

The second set-back, coming a few minutes later, was more daunting, since the next dish set before them was slices of raw tuna fish covered, but not concealed, by a blanket of black sauce. The pleasure with which the men beside them greeted this delicacy did nothing to dispel Epifanio's almost tangible disgust, but Imeldo, as usual, rose handsomely to the occasion. Smiling stiffly with feigned enjoyment, forcing himself to eat a few small pieces of a substance he had sworn would never again cross his lips, he then explained in extravagant mime that his poor shrunken stomach was not yet ready to do justice to such a banquet. Honour was satisfied, and the two survivors returned to their cabin to rest and to consider their future.

Although both of them at first fretted over the delay in restoring them to their families, long before that reunion took place they were to change their outlook completely. The enforced delay gave them the chance to learn a thing or two about a world beyond their horizons and by the time they next set foot upon the island of their birth both Imeldo and Epifanio had decided and agreed upon a policy of reticence and near-silence that they were to adhere to for several years to come.

The explanation of this self-imposed secrecy is in no way sinister, but merely in accord with Imeldo's and Epifanio's upbringing in a peasant society where interference by outsiders is traditionally regarded with suspicion. Two essentially simple men, they found themselves, during the next few days, transformed into celebrities, their privacy and most personal thoughts no longer their own. They simply decided, swiftly and with increasing vehemence, that they did not enjoy the experience.

But first there were happier moments in store. Early on the morning of 20 January they were roused from sleep and ushered on deck to join the captain, smiling broadly and pointing for'ard over the prow of his ship. Within seconds his smile and those of the crewmen around him had changed to uproarious laughter, for at that instant Imeldo and Epifanio went berserk.

Small wonder, for what confronted them this time was no mirage. The first solid ground they had seen for three dreadful weeks was a green and lovely island, the biggest of the Palau group, and the trees that fringed its glittering white beaches were welcoming and real.

As the men of the *Hachi-Ho-Maru No. 6* clustered chattering around them, preparing to say farewell, the two men from Tenerife watched with tears in their eyes the sweeping approach of a gleaming motor launch manned by a native civilian and by a captain of the United States Air Force who jumped nimbly aboard the trawler and spoke amicably, in fluent Japanese, to her skipper. Within minutes, in a flurry of hurried farewells, Imeldo Barreto Léon and Epifanio Perdomo López stepped on to the deck of the motor launch, at the start of the long journey home.

On shore it seemed that both the islanders and the American military had declared the day a festival, and men, women and children stood waving and cheering as soldiers ran down to the beach bearing stretchers to carry the guests of honour to their headquarters nearby. Epifanio was lifted up and laid gently on one canvas litter but Imeldo, head high, strode ashore without assistance. Proud, certainly, but not arrogant, for his very next action was to kneel down and kiss the ground.

'That's exactly how I feel too,' said Epifanio wistfully, 'but my legs have gone at last, and I just know I could never get down on my knees and up again.'

Without a word Imeldo scooped up a handful of sand and carried it across to his shipmate, and without prompting the soldiers and the villagers, even the children, fell silent as the second of the survivors payed his homage, too, to whatever Power had brought them through to safety at last.

They were to remain on the island for no more than a few hours, but within that short time they were to experience warmth and kindness that neither will ever forget. As doctors dressed Epifanio's injuries, gifts poured in – clothing and money and chocolate and cigarettes from soldiers and civilians alike – and only minutes before they were taken aboard an aeroplane for the flight to Okinawa, a native in working clothes ran forward to press upon each of them five dollars of his hard-earned wage – 'to buy a drink in remembrance of their visit'. It was scarcely one they were likely to forget.

The hours then spent on Okinawa proved much less to their liking, and it was during this time that they began to develop a mistrustful resentment of total strangers who seemed to regard them not as human beings in a distressed condition, but as the property of anyone who chose to lay claim, often rudely, upon their time and their attention. Their initial reception by the United States Air Force in Okinawa was friendly, hospitable and considerate – but Imeldo and Epifanio were now celebrities, protagonists of a drama in which the Services had played a prominent part, and it would have been neither feasible nor reasonable to refuse conference facilities to the assembled press corps and TV crews who had gathered in strength.

They were there in their dozens, and it was ordeal enough for two men in such a weakened state to have to face them as they shouted, jostled, fired flash-bulbs and thrust out microphones. But to add to the bewilderment of two characters utterly unused to being stared at and hounded for 'quotes' – incredibly, out of all the journalists gathered there at huge expense, not one spoke a single word of Spanish. The hubbub engulfing them was not just deafening: it was totally incomprehensible.

The reporters, however, were insistent and by using a mixture of sign-language and broken English they subjected Imeldo and Epifanio to an interrogation regarding the circumstances of the *Istra*'s sinking, an inquisition yielding little more than that she had gone down after three explosions, that the end had come almost within seconds, and that there had been no sign of any other survivors. Despite this and the fact that three weeks had now elapsed since the disaster, the United States Air Force, to their credit, sent out eight more aircraft the next day for one final search. They traced the oil slick that the raft had crossed, reporting it as ninety miles long and two miles wide, and they circled the sea for a hundred miles all round it, but there was no sign of further life and the air-sea rescue operation, the biggest ever mounted, was finally abandoned.

In London the sinking had already been acknowledged at Lloyd's by the striking of the Lutine Bell, only the second time in thirty years that such action had been taken to confirm the loss of a vessel previously reported missing. One stroke on the bell had been sounded by the Lloyd's caller, Mr Alex Barnard, and the sinking had been recorded in the Loss Book by Mr David Burling. It was announced at the same time that the London Market would bear seventy per cent of the $18 million on the hull, and the whole of a further $9 million in total loss interest, figures that, big as they sound to the layman, caused no great ripples on the tranquil surface of the insurance ocean.

'There are plenty of vessels of this size at sea,' remarked Mr Charles Gibb, a leading marine insurance underwriter and Chairman of the Lloyd's Underwriters Association. 'The fact that one goes down does not imply any drastic change in rates. The Hamburg floods three weeks ago will probably cost underwriters more than this.'

On 21 January Imeldo and Epifanio were flown to Tokyo, where money and new passports were provided for them by the Spanish Embassy, and the following day they began a zig-zag journey across oceans and continents which led them to a world they had never known, an environment that disturbed and frightened them almost as badly as had the floating hell from which they had so recently escaped.

From Tokyo they were flown to Copenhagen via Alaska. Next, to their utter bewilderment and dismay, instead of being taken home to Tenerife they were flown to New York and incarcerated in an hotel for almost a week, where they were subjected to protracted interrogation by officials of the Republic of Liberia, in whose country the *Berge Istra* had been registered under a flag of convenience.

The questions put to them concerned not only the timing and location of the three explosions but also such matters as the exact nature of their own duties, and whether they worked alone or under an officer's supervision. All this seemed natural enough, but what Imeldo and Epifanio found disquieting was a subsequent series of questions asking, for example, whether at Tubarao they had noticed the loading of any cargo other than iron ore. This line of enquiry sounded ominously like a police or customs investigation, and they insisted that they were simple seamen carrying out mundane tasks, that they had no concern with the administration relating to ship or cargo, and that, furthermore, during several hours of the loading operation they had been off duty enjoying themselves on shore.

This identification of themselves as 'simple seamen', with its implicit suggestion of ignorance on matters concerning the day-to-day running of the *Berge Istra*, was one that they were to maintain to a greater or lesser degree throughout all subsequent enquiries. Later, when asked why, they replied reasonably enough that it was no business of theirs to comment upon the orders or actions of their superiors and that they had no wish to make any critical remarks that might conceivably endanger either their own future employment or the granting of compensation to the families of their dead comrades. Liberian officials and persistent journalists alike found to their chagrin that these two dour men from the Canaries, despite their dangerous adventures, did not make good copy.

It was not until they had spent four days in New York that

they were handed over to the Spanish Embassy, who understandably were less than delighted at the delay. They had been virtually under siege all week as Spanish-speaking media men protested furiously that the Hispanic public in their millions were waiting eagerly for first-hand accounts of shipwreck and disaster on the high seas. The Liberian interrogation, the Embassy suggested, could surely have been postponed at least until the survivors had been given the chance to send messages of reassurance to their families.

At last the wrangling and recriminations were over, and accompanied by Sig. Bergesen's agent Imeldo and Epifanio were flown to Madrid to face another press conference, a noisy, confusing and exhausting ritual they were already growing to hate. Escape came with the announcement of their flight to Las Palmas, and although there were more reporters there, too, with more cameras and more questions, mercifully the stop-over lasted only thirty minutes and then, at last, they found themselves on the final leg of the journey home.

Their reception in Tenerife was tumultuous; everyone, it seemed, from both Taganana and Punta de Hidalgo was there to greet them. As they came down the gangway they were lifted off their feet and carried shoulder-high by shouting supporters across the airport to where their families stood waiting. The kissing, hugging and laughter for once held all but the most insensitive reporters at bay.

The press, frantic for at least some semblance of a story to grace the next editions, eventually persuaded them to go into the VIP lounge for yet another conference, but by this time the weary heroes had had enough. They wanted no more questions – their one wish was to forget both the *Berge Istra* and their ordeal. As far as they were concerned it was all now thankfully in the past and they wanted to be left alone with their nearest and dearest.

The press, reluctantly, took the point, and family and friends took over. Imeldo, Epifanio, their wives and their children were bundled into a fleet of private cars and driven ceremoniously to their homes. Motor horns blared all the way, folk rushed from their houses to wave and to cheer them as they passed. For their friends the occasion would soon become a joyous fiesta that would last far into the night, but for the two men at the centre of it all it was now time for quiet, for reflection, and for an inner happiness that neither one of them had ever known before.

It was many, many months before Imeldo and Epifanio were to meet each other again, except on formal or official occasions. But time gradually healed their wounds. Meeting occasionally on a Sunday to walk on the beach or the cliff-tops they found that their differences had faded, and Imeldo became godfather to David, Epifanio's youngest son.

APPENDIX I

Observer 18 January 1976

SUDDEN DEATH OF A GIANT TANKER

BY IAN MATHER

The *Berge Istra*, a Norwegian-owned supertanker dwarfing the *Titanic* and the biggest ship ever to vanish, probably broke in half and sank in three minutes in one of the deepest seas in the world.

The theory of 'sudden death' has emerged as the most likely explanation of one of the weirdest mysteries in maritime history.

Most people in the shipping world now believe the vessel is lying six miles down in the Mindanao Trench, east of the Philippines. The exact truth may never be known, for there is little hope of a proper investigation at that depth.

The *Berge Istra* was a 'combination' tanker of 224,000 tons (the *Titanic* was 46,000 tons) capable of carrying oil or ore. She sailed from the Brazilian port of Tubarao on 29 November with 188,000 tons of iron ore bound for Tokyo Bay, where she should have arrived on 5 January. She was last reported on course south-west of Mindanao, the southernmost island of the Philippines, on 29 December. Then she vanished.

Her fate has been the subject of intense debate among shipping experts. Any reasonable theory must answer three baffling questions:

Why did she not send out a distress signal?

Why has not a single scrap of floating debris been spotted in the massive search of over 300,000 square miles of ocean that has been going on since the owners raised the alarm?

The search has now been called off.

Modern supertankers are so huge and have so much reserve buoyancy (air space inside the hull) that the chances of them sinking are very slight.

The *Berge Istra* was a modern ship, built in 1972 by a reputable Yugoslav company, Uljanik of Pula. She carried a 100 A1 certificate of seaworthiness, the highest rating, from Norske Veritas, the Norwegian equivalent of Lloyd's

Her Norwegian owners, Sig. Bergesen DY, have an international reputation for safety, having lost only one ship in forty years, and that during the last war. Her captain was an experienced Norwegian seaman.

Yet all clues to the tanker's fate have proved false. The US Navy picked up what they thought was a garbled message saying a survivor had been spotted on a small Pacific island. The message proved to be incorrect. Then a search aircraft spotted lights on an island thought to be uninhabited. But a plane flying over the island at daybreak found a previously unmapped village.

The mystery has produced a spate of imaginative theories, including piracy and hijacking. Her alternative captain, Tor Gudmundsen, waiting in vain in Tokyo to take over the vessel, has apparently not ruled out piracy. 'The ship is green and if you sailed into an inlet with it, it would be difficult to spot in all that greenery,' he said. But such a theory appears fanciful. It is hard to imagine what pirates would hope to do with their booty of 188,000 tons of iron ore, and the ship itself could hardly be slipped on to the second-hand market without anyone noticing.

A political hijacking must probably be ruled out, too. The South Moluccan nationalist movement, which made its appearance with the train hijack in Holland last month and which is dedicated to home rule for a section of Indonesia, has been suggested.

So have Philippine Muslim guerrillas, who last year hijacked some small ships near Mindanao. But hijackers would either have communicated their demands to the world by now, or the ship's whereabouts would surely have been discovered.

All the more reasonable theories hinge on some sort of disaster in the ship itself. An explosion on board could have knocked out the radio but would not have caused the ship to disappear. Modern tankers are built in water-tight compartments, and at this moment a P and O tanker is sailing back to Britain with its engine room totally flooded. The *Berge Istra* would have been able to contact passing ships through emergency radios provided for her life-rafts.

An electrical failure, too, would not have prevented the ship making it to port, and again, auxiliary radios would have been used. If the ship had broken up on a reef, or had sunk slowly, there would have been time for the radio operator to send out a May-day signal and there would have been a vast amount of floating debris.

So shipping experts are led to the conclusion that the *Berge Istra* sank suddenly. There are two ways in which this can happen to giant tankers. According to one captain, if a tanker were to 'turn turtle' or break in half while carrying a heavy solid cargo, the crew would have only three minutes to get off before she sank like a stone.

Of the two theories, the less likely one is that the tanker turned turtle. This can happen in certain circumstances which do not apply to the *Berge Istra*. A vessel is in danger of turning over if it is partly loaded with certain types of cargo in the bottom of the hold. The distribution of weight can set up forces similar to those of the wind acting on a stone tied to the end of a string. The motion of the sea can set up a pendulum effect which can ultimately cause a ship to list beyond the point of recovery.

This is likely to happen only if the cargo moves, and iron ore is a 'safe' cargo from this point of view. But iron ore *would* be a potentially lethal cargo to a ship like the *Berge Istra* (as long as three football pitches) if it were not loaded with great care, and if it were only a partial cargo.

The ore has to be loaded into the ship's holds in equal quantities to balance the weight. It this is not done, and some holds are full while others are empty, the ship's hull, especially over a long voyage, can be strained to breaking point, even without a storm. The action of the swell would be enough to split the ship in half and the in-rush of the sea would cause her to sink very quickly.

Though weather reports from the US Air Force base at Kadena, Okinawa, where the search has been co-ordinated, indicate that sea conditions were good, there were tropical storms in the North Pacific and the ripple effect from these would produce rollers over a wide area.

If the *Berge Istra* had been carrying a full load it would automatically have been evenly distributed. But she was carrying only half her capacity.

So the theory that the ship was wrongly loaded at the Brazilian port of Tubarao, either through negligence or language difficulties, is the most likely explanation for the tragedy.

The absence of debris is explained by the fact that the more quickly a ship sinks the less wreckage she leaves on the surface. Modern tankers, unlike modern liners, have no deck furniture. Unlike many other ships, they have no rigging.

The fear of a vessel snapping in two is, in fact, the nightmare of some masters of very long tankers. A supertanker built by Harland and Wolff broke clean in two during trials in the North Sea. The tremendous depth of the Mindanao Trench would have caused 'implosion'. As the hull sank the build-up of water pressure would have forced her mass together, until she arrived at the bottom like a squashed sardine tin.

What little debris there may have been would have been widely scattered by the time the search began. There was a delay of several days because the last 'contact' with the ship was in fact merely a computer read-out of her projected position; the *Berge Istra* was being 'weather-routed' – following a computerized course set for her and automatically modified for her by weather stations.

This leaves the final problem of the missing distress signal. This can be explained if the ship did sink in three minutes.

According to international rules, modified on 1 January, the ship's radio would have to be manned for only eight hours in each twenty-four-hour period, for four hours in the morning, two in the evening, and for two more hours according to the captain's instructions.

When the radio is not manned, an alarm system alerts the crew to an *incoming* signal But the radio officer would not normally be in the radio room. During a long, boring voyage, he could be asleep, in the swimming pool, or having a meal. Or he could be a quarter of a mile away at the bow of the ship. It is normal for tanker crews on long journeys to take regular exercise by walking round the ship.

In the event of a sudden disaster, the radio officer might have been unable or too preoccupied to reach the radio room. Or he might not have had time to activate the transmitter (assuming it was in working order) and obtain instructions from the bridge, before the ship went down.

The loss of the *Berge Istra* will involve a pay-out of £10 million by Lloyds of London where the ship was insured for 70 per cent of its value. The loss will be borne by several thousand underwriters and is unlikely to strain the marine insurance market, though underwriters could be seen last week anxiously scanning the latest intelligence bulletins about the ship, pinned to the notice board in Lloyds main hall.

The *Berge Istra*, while likely to become the biggest shipping loss, will cost Lloyds less than the Hamburg floods two weeks ago and only a fraction of the Darwin floods last year. But the ritual ringing of the Lutine Bell signifying the death of a ship is unlikely to take place. The bell is rung only when a loss is confirmed through wreckage or survivors, or when a ship reappears, in which case the bell is rung twice. The *Berge Istra* is likely to remain simply a missing ship unrecorded in Lloyds loss book. The pay-out takes place after a 'reasonable' period of time – about three months.

Daily Express 19 January 1976

BY ASHLEY WALTON

Two crewmen from the vanished supertanker *Berge Istra* have been picked up alive after twenty days adrift on a life-raft.

And they have solved the £14 million mystery of the biggest shipwreck in history: it was ripped apart by three explosions.

The rescue by a Japanese fishing boat revives hopes of saving more of the crew of thirty-two including a Briton.

An air and sea search – abandoned last week – was being resumed at dawn today.

The 224,000-ton *Berge Istra* vanished at the end of December on a voyage from Brazil to Japan.

According to a message from the Japanese boat, *Hachihou Maru*, the survivors said they were painting on deck when disaster struck. There was no explanation for the blasts.

Their rescue just before midnight on Saturday was revealed by Tokyo yesterday.

The unidentified men were reported to be in good condition after twenty days adrift in the Pacific before being saved about 700 miles south-east of Mindanao Island in the Philippines.

Their ship, insured for about £14 million by its Norwegian owners, was 100 miles south-west of the island when it sent its last radio report on 29 December.

After that . . . silence. The three-year-old *Berge Istra* – 1,029 ft long and carrying 180,000 tons of iron ore – never arrived in Tokyo on 5 January as scheduled.

US Air Force planes based in Okinawa and the Philippines searched for a week.

Sig. Bergesen DY, the ship's Oslo owners, began paying compensation to the crew's relatives.

Thirteen of the crew were from Norway, twelve from the Spanish Tenerife Islands, two from Belgium, two from Yugoslavia, and one each from Brazil, Britain and Sweden.

The Briton is radio officer Ronald Lemarche, aged thirty-four from Bluestone Hill, Alderney, in the Channel Islands.

His wife's stepfather, Mr Eric White, said: 'Sandra has become reconciled to the thought that he is dead – and now these two unidentified crewmen are found alive. She is very distressed at the moment.'

She is staying with relatives in Warminster, Wiltshire.

Mr Lemarche gave up the sea five years ago to make a living fishing off Alderney. But it did not pay and he went back to his old career three years later.

Remains of the stricken tanker could now be at the bottom of the awesome Mindanao Trench, six and a half miles deep.

About seventy per cent of its insurance cover is held by Lloyd's of London who face a £10 million bill – their biggest ever shipping loss.

Sun 19 January 1976

BLASTED OUT OF THE SEA!
BY DENIS BUDGE

A giant ship that vanished in the Pacific – causing one of the greatest sea mysteries of all time – was destroyed by a series of explosions, it was revealed last night.

Two surprise survivors from the Norwegian tanker *Berge Istra*, which was bigger than the doomed liner *Titanic*, said their ship went down after three massive blasts on 29 December.

A Japanese fishing boat picked up the pair from a life-raft north of New Guinea after twenty days adrift.

They told how they were painting on the deck of the 224,000-ton ship – built to carry oil and other bulk cargoes – when the explosions occurred.

They are believed to have swum to a raft blown clear by the blasts.

The 32-strong crew of the *Berge Istra* is believed to have included three women. The radio operator was a Briton, Roger Le Marche, from Alderney in the Channel Islands.

He apparently had no time to send out a distress signal.

The ship was on its way from Brazil to Japan carrying 180,000 tons of iron ore.

The mystery that remains is what caused the blasts.

One expert said last night that the explanation could be pockets of gas, which remained from a previous oil cargo.

The last radio message heard from the *Berge Istra* was when it was 100 miles off Mindanao Island in the Philippines.

Operator Le Marche said the ship would be arriving at Kimitsu, Japan, on 5 January.

The rescue of the two men is likely to start a new search for other possible survivors.

In London today the 200-year-old Lutine bell will be rung at Lloyd's – signalling the biggest ever pay-out in shipping insurance.

The £10 million loss will be borne by several thousand underwriters in Britain and Norway.

Times 22 January 1976

SURVIVORS FROM ORE CARRIER VOW NEVER TO GO TO SEA AGAIN

Kadena Base, Okinawa. 21 Jan. – Two Spanish seamen, the sole survivors from the crew of thirty-two of the Norwegian supertanker *Berge Istra* which vanished in the western Pacific, tonight swore never to go to sea again.

Señor Epifanio Perdomo López, aged thirty-seven, a father of nine with a new-born son he has not yet seen, said: 'I would prefer to go begging before I go back to a ship.' He and Señor Imeldo Barreto Léon, aged forty-one, were giving their first full account at an American forces base of the fate of the 227,556-ton ore and oil carrier which disappeared without trace three weeks ago.

The two men, both from Tenerife in the Canary Islands, told of three explosions, one of which almost capsized the ship. Señor López said he was on deck at the time fully clothed, but the explosion ripped off everything but his undershirt.

Then their nineteen long days of misery began, adrift on a life-raft, eating raw fish and drinking rainwater – praying, they said, for a miracle or an angel to save them.

Officials at the rescue centre at Kadena tonight called off a search for further survivors after hearing their story. The *Berge Istra* was last heard from on 29 December southwest of Mindanao island in the Philippines while on a voyage from Brazil to Japan.

The two seamen said they were in a group of four scraping paint at the bow of the ship at about 4.45 p.m. on 30 December when they heard something resembling a rush of air, followed immediately by an explosion.

Speaking through an interpreter, they told a press conference how two more explosions shook the ship, sending it to the bottom within about three minutes. Escaping from the whirlpool as the ship went down, they scrambled into a life-raft. It contained rations and water for ten days and when these ran out they depended on what they could catch.

Twice they spotted ships as they drifted across the Pacific

but it was not until three days ago that a Japanese tuna fishing vessel took them on board.

The two explained how the second explosion, though apparently smaller than the first, seemed to open the ship and almost capsized it. They had finished untying the raft when there was a third explosion on the starboard side as the ship sank.

Señor López said: 'I was hanging on and water was on my feet and the next thing I remember is being in a whirlpool.' That was the last thing he recalled until he revived on the raft.

Señor Léon, father of three girls and a boy, also remembered being sucked into a whirlpool. When he surfaced there was nothing to be seen of the ship but debris.

He pulled Señor López on to the raft and revived him with mouth-to-mouth resuscitation. He thought: 'Now I have a friend.'

The raft was so low in the water that bailing was a constant chore. At night they were struck by cold. They caught fish on a line in the survival kit and rainwater in a canvas sheet. After rescue Señor López was so overcome he could hardly eat but Señor Léon 'ate enough for the two of them'. Señor López, who sat in a hospital wheelchair with bandaged legs, and his companion were earlier examined by an American Air Force doctor who pronounced them in good shape considering their ordeal. Each lost about 22 lb.

Mr Stang Lund, a Norwegian lawyer representing the ship's owners, vetted the questions put to the survivors and refused to allow them to reply about possibilities of sabotage. – Reuter, AP and UPI.

APPENDIX II

REPUBLIC OF LIBERIA

DECISION OF THE COMMISSIONER
OF MARITIME AFFAIRS, R. L.
and
REPORT
of the
MARINE BOARD OF INVESTIGATION

In the Matter of the Explosion and Sinking
of
THE M/S BERGE ISTRA (O.N. 4168)
on 30 DECEMBER 1975

PUBLISHED BY THE BUREAU OF MARITIME
AFFAIRS
by Authority of the
MINISTER OF FINANCE

31 MARCH 1978
Monrovia, Liberia

REPUBLIC OF LIBERIA
MINISTRY OF FINANCE
MONROVIA, LIBERIA

OFFICE OF THE COMMISSIONER
FOR MARITIME AFFAIRS

Decision of the Commissioner of Maritime Affairs
in the Matter of the Sinking of the
M/S BERGE ISTRA (O.N. 4168)
in the Pacific Ocean on 30 December, 1975

Authority

This decision is rendered pursuant to the provisions of Sections 11, 18 and 258 of the Liberian Maritime Law, and Liberian Maritime Regulation 9.258(7).

Comment

On 30 December 1975, between four and five o'clock in the afternoon in the Molucca Sea, the motor combination carrier BERGE ISTRA suffered a rapid series of massive explosions in its aft section which resulted to immediate sinking and the loss of life of all but two of her thirty-two member crew. The vessel was carrying a cargo of 188,208 metric tons of high grade iron ore from Tubarao, Brazil to Kimitsu, Japan. The two survivors drifted aboard a life-raft until picked up by a fishing vessel on 17 January, 1976.

A Preliminary Investigation was convened on 28 January, 1976 in accordance with Liberian Maritime Regulation 9.252. Based on the recommendation of the report of this investigation the undersigned directed the appointment of a Marine

Board of Investigation to probe the cause of the casualty. The Board held a formal hearing in London from 21 through 30 June, 1976, and submitted the attached report as its Final Report.

The undersigned, having reviewed the Report of the Board of Investigation, notes the following:
- There are various possibilities which could be put forward as the cause of the explosions that resulted in the sinking of the vessel, but equally, all are beset with difficulties and improbabilities. The definitive cause of the explosions that sank the BERGE ISTRA must therefore remain, at least for the present, one of the unsolved mysteries of the sea.
- Since one of the primary objectives of such investigation is preventive, the undersigned is of the opinion that all of the possible causes of the disaster should be given the fullest consideration in future safety design and construction of vessels.

1. To the recommendations contained in paragraph 48 (2) are added the recommendations that IMCO be invited to consider
   (g) any special measures which may be advisable to ensure that all void spaces are and remain gas free during a dry cargo voyage following an oil voyage, and
   (h) whether in future combination carriers, a cofferdam should be provided between bunker and dry cargo tanks.

2. As to the comments of the Board at the conclusion of paragraph 35 concerning the liferaft construction and provisioning, and the Board's recommendation in paragraph 48 (4) for IMCO consideration of improving liferaft requirements, it seems worth noting that the Liberian requirement for the forward 6-man liferaft which in fact saved the BERGE ISTRA survivors is in excess of the international requirements. In

theory, such a raft is intended to enable men trapped forward to escape and await pickup by their own ship's boats; it is not intended to support life at sea for 18 days, even in undamaged condition. While this raft was suitable for its intended purpose, it is open for consideration by IMCO whether such a raft is sufficient in the overall future plan of lifesaving appliances aboard ships such as the BERGE ISTRA.

ACTION

1. With the comments above, the Report of the Marine Board of Investigation and its findings, conclusions and recommendations are hereby adopted in full and directed to be published together with this decision.

2. On behalf of the Bureau of Maritime Affairs, profound gratitude and appreciation is expressed to the United States Coast Guard, the United States Air Force, the Japanese Maritime Safety Agency and to the various vessels, aircraft and ground personnel who cooperated in conducting the vast search efforts for BERGE ISTRA survivors.

3. With great pleasure it is requested that the Ministry of Foreign Affairs, R.L. send an official letter of thanks through diplomatic channels to the Owners, Master and Crew of the fishing vessel HACHIMO MARU, attesting their humanitarian service rendered to the survivors.

4. With great pleasure an appropriate commendation will go forward from the Bureau of Maritime Affairs to IMELDO BORRETO LÉON, attesting his valor in rescuing Epifanio Perdomo López, his seamanship during 18 days aboard the raft, and his willing cooperation in this investigation, all in the highest traditions of the sea.

5. In view of the particular importance which this casualty has with relation to the continuing quest for improving safety

of life and property at sea, copies of the Decision and Report will be transmitted to the Inter-Governmental Maritime Consultative Organization for consideration, directing particular attention to paragraphs 1 and 2 of this Decision and paragraph 48 (2) to (6) of the Report.

6. As to paragraph 48 (7) and (8) of the Report, these are remitted to the Senior Deputy Commissioner and to the Admiralty Counsel of the Bureau of Maritime Affairs, respectively, for implementation.

Done at Monrovia, Montserrado County, Republic of Liberia, this 10th day of March, A.D. 1978.

Gerald F. B. Cooper
COMMISSIONER OF MARITIME AFFAIRS, R.L.

Excerpts from the Remaining Part of the Report

(The page numbers at the end of each excerpt refer to the relevant passages in the text of this book.)

18. The Board was favourably impressed by the evidence of Captain Botnen, Captain Gudmundsen, and Mr Hofseth [Previous masters and chief engineer of the BERGE ISTRA], who appeared to be men of great professional competence. It seems fair to assume that the officers serving in the BERGE ISTRA at the time of her loss were of similar professional competence, and the Board sees no reason to take any view but that she was well and competently manned. So far as concerns the maintenance of the vessel and her equipment,

and the employment of qualified and trained personnel, the Board sees no reason to criticize her Owners and Managers. (Pages 3, 4.)

25. The reason given for preferring to gas-free the tanks after cleaning, rather than re-inerting them, was that the Riken instrument [an explosimeter] would not record an accurate hydro-carbon content in the presence of inert gas. It appears to the Board, however, that this does give rise to the possibility of tanks gassing up, either from undetected residues or from gas or oil leakage back from the slop tank. (Pages 17–18.)

27. But it would appear that there is a greater margin of safety in inerting, as compared with gas-freeing, since a large amount of free air is required to bring a properly inerted tank into the flammable range, whereas in the case of gas-freeing only a small percentage of hydro-carbon vapour is needed to produce a mixture above the lower flammable limit. For these reasons it appears to the Board that the course which was probably adopted in the case of the BERGE ISTRA may be of doubtful wisdom, and that it is for consideration whether combination carriers of this size and type, when engaged in carrying dry cargo, should always be required to have their empty tanks inerted. (Pages 17, 18, 23.)

28. One strange feature of the case is that during this voyage the BERGE ISTRA made no attempt to participate in the 'AMVER' system. This abbreviation stands for 'Automated Mutual Assistance Vessel Rescue System', and the system is operated free of charge by the United States Coastguard. A participating ship has only to transmit at intervals (free of charge) coded messages giving her position, and also to notify changes of course or speed. This information is fed into a computer which is thus able to predict what the ship's position will be at any given time. On previous voyages the BERGE ISTRA had always participated, and what ren-

ders her failure to participate on this voyage all the more surprising is that her Master, Captain Hemnes, had the reputation of being an Amver 'fan' and had an impressive record of participation in the past. (Pages 30, 54, 55, 57, 63.)

36. In the meantime nobody knew until the 5th January 1976 that any casualty had occurred. On that day the Owners received a message from their agents in Japan informing them that the BERGE ISTRA had not arrived. On the same day the Norwegian radio station reported that the Owners' radio messages to the vessel on the 31st December had not been delivered. It has already been mentioned that it was customary for the BERGE ISTRA to transmit a routine radio message every Wednesday. It is matter for comment that nobody in the Owners' office appears to have noticed the non-receipt of any such message on Wednesday, the 31st of December, and nobody appears to have been concerned until the report of the vessel's non-arrival was received on the 5th January, 1976. (Pages 52, 53, 54, 63.)

40. There was no evidence whatsoever to point to the possibility of any external cause of the explosions. It would not be reasonable, for instance, to infer that the vessel had struck a floating mine left over from the last War. Nor is there any ground for suspecting any form of sabotage. The Board is satisfied that the cause or causes of the disaster must be sought within the vessel herself. (Pages 2, 3.)

APPENDIX III

Psychiatric Report on Imeldo Barreto Léon

Mr Barreto is a somewhat reserved individual and before venturing any information he queried the reason for this test and asked what it was to be used for.

He has a low standard of general knowledge as he only completed a minimum amount of schooling, but he subsequently learnt to read and write through his own efforts. He has always been an introvert with a tendency towards isolation and is not fond of amusements.

He had a hard childhood due to precarious family circumstances and from a very early age was compelled to work and assume the responsibilities of a much older person. In my view this proved a decisive factor in his own and his companion's survival following the shipwreck, as he was able to take on his shoulders the task of caring for his injured companion and providing means of subsistence throughout the time they spent on the raft. His introvert nature, little given to extremes of emotion, helped him to keep calm except at critical moments, when a depressive reaction set in, coupled with the idea of committing suicide, and it is very likely that he would have gone through with his plan had he been alone. Apart from survival his main preoccupation at the time was the thought of his companions who died when the ship sank, and this pre-occupation remains with him still.

Mr Imeldo Barreto has a fairly stable personality and an intelligence far exceeding his general standard of education. He is also fully aware of his commitments towards his family and society.

The Machover test confirmed the clinical impression, highlighting his lack of confidence in social relationships and his timid nature. It also confirmed his capacity to assume responsibility and a certain degree of mistrust.

The severe psychological stress to which he was subjected as a result of the shipwreck left him in a depressed condition which has still failed to disappear after three years, although it has fluctuated to some extent. This clinical pattern is mainly characterized by ill-humour, lack of concentration, sleeplessness and a tendency towards excessive worry. His condition could be successfully treated from a clinical standpoint, but its long-term effects are impossible to predict.

SANTA CRUZ DE TENERIFE, 23 February 1979
A. Garcia-Estrada Perez, Psychiatrist

Graphological Study of Imeldo's Personality

We are faced with a subject who, in addition to receiving a scanty education, lived in an environment which afforded him little opportunity to gain experience.

His view of reality, within a general or synoptic context, is lacking in clarity as he has no sense of proportion. Judgements involve comparing minor details, but they are ingenious nevertheless. To arrive at essentials he uses a simple, uncomplicated reasoning process, but one based on clear and precise notions. For instance, he distinguishes men from women by their hair – a woman's hair is long, a man's hair short – without taking into account any other factors. This shows that he has a basically analytical mind, in that he does not see the overall view but only details.

His thoughts range from logical to idealistic.

Logic usually prevails. In new or unexpected situations exceeding the bounds of routine and acquired habit – from which he usually obtains guidance in human problems – he always takes decisions based on past experience. Where logic fails, his lack of comprehension makes him act on the basis of external impressions – he is a very impressionable person – which he interprets according to their positive or negative effect on his emotions: anything pleasing is good, anything displeasing is bad. In such situations he acts instinctively, guiding himself by ideas instead of searching in his mind.

He has difficulty in adapting to different environments, particularly where people are involved, and prefers others to adapt themselves to his way. Where he fails to achieve this he tends to isolate himself, seeking comfort in solitude. He prefers to be alone, surrounded by things he recognizes as his own – objects, working materials, nature, etc – and by his family. He is a very independent person.

Imeldo is inclined to be timid, unsure of himself when faced with other people and with the future. He is self-analytical and thinks out problems in his mind but never reaches firm conclusions about what to do in a particular situation. He cannot adopt a specific and definitive attitude towards the world around him, or towards things and people.

He lacks fighting spirit and decision, preferring to withdraw to an environment where he feels secure, within a family setting.

Unable to make his way in the world of reality he lives spiritually. His sensitive nature supports and complements his spiritual existence. In relations with his wife and children he displays an idealized outlook which compensates for his lack of achievement and success in life.

Imeldo's reservedness is the result of a very strong inhibition in the face of situations and problems originating outside his own surroundings. This causes a tendency towards discouragement, lack of self-confidence and a feeling of hopelessness.

His extremely rigid ego expresses itself in an excessive morality, and this should be regarded as a very valuable asset considering the fact that he is an uneducated person.

Temperamentally he is lymphatic with an underlying bilious prevalence. He is mild but irascible, touchy and suspicious. He becomes irritated if opposed, and particularly when his word is doubted.

INTELLECTUAL CAPACITY

Virtually uneducated, Imeldo acquires knowledge by analysis. He has trouble seeing things in their overall perspective. His judgements are good, insofar as his assessment of specific details is concerned, and are based on sound common sense. He describes details in an ingenious manner. His ideas are clear and precise, provided he is dealing with specific details. His understanding has a logical basis and involves establishing comparisons with situations experienced in the past. However, because of his tendency towards isolation and lack of contact with others his experience is scarce and, in a crisis, he clings to two or three ideas which serve him as a guide: God, the image of his wife and children, etc. In other words, he has an idealistic mind governed by ideas and not by concepts, as previously described.

MORAL STANDARDS

Imeldo can clearly distinguish one thing from another. He knows what is 'yours' and what is 'mine'. He has a great respect for other people's property, is faithful, honest, prudent to a degree bordering on mistrust, sincere and has an inborn spiritual sensitivity. He idealizes his wife and children. But he is over-scrupulous.

PSYCHIATRIC DIAGNOSIS AID

Although the documents produced before the shipwreck are insufficient to ensure comprehensive graphological assessment, it can be deduced that Imeldo suffers from a very marked inhibitory tendency or, to be more precise, a general state of inhibition of the faculties which particularly affects his psychomotility. It should be explained that this condition already existed prior to the shipwreck, although it was not so severe then as at the present time. Consequently, since the shipwreck his inhibitions have taken a turn for the worse, with all that this implies.

From a psycho-analytical viewpoint account should be taken of his demanding ego, a fixation on his mother and an ambivalent attitude towards his father, two entirely contrary sentiments towards the parental image.

His excessively rigid and demanding ego, over-scrupulousness and a tendency to examine his conscience to see whether he has acted rightly, often lead to self-reproach. Aggressiveness towards others generates a feeling of guilt which turns against him (introjection of aggressiveness) and manifests itself as a masochistic tendency.

He has intrapunitive sentiments and an (unconscious?) desire to mortify himself, to 'kill himself off slowly' (he should be very careful as regards the use of drugs).

At present, ie subsequent to the shipwreck, he is deeply troubled and low-spirited, beset by scruples, a guilt complex, obsession and a pre-occupation with the world beyond.

Moments of hope alternate with discouragement, pessimism and anguish, but discouragement and a feeling of helplessness prevail over hope. Momentary hope (euphoria) gives way to depression, which has an element of exitability or nervousness.

In short, we are faced with a schizoid subject whose natural or constitutional tendency to isolate his private life from society by avoiding any attempt to establish contact with others has developed as a result of circumstances.

I certainly feel that he should undergo psychotherapy.

Given at Santa Cruz de Tenerife on the 10th day of February nineteen hundred and seventy nine.

Signed

CHAIRMAN OF THE CANARIAN-VENEZUELAN SOCIETY OF GRAPHOLOGY AND PSYCHOLOGY

Psychiatric Report on Epifanio Perdomo López

Mr Perdomo is a very frank individual who answered all the questions put to him without any hesitation whatsoever.

From a study of his background it appears that he had what can be termed a normal childhood, except that he lost his mother at a very early age and this became a crucial factor in the development of his personal relationships.

He went to school until the age of thirteen and obtained a primary school certificate without too much difficulty.

He married at the age of twenty and almost immediately began to have differences with his wife as he was always going out to amuse himself and paid little attention to the home or the children. His relations with women other than his wife were frequent but always superficial and short-lived, being the expression of an immature character which reflected itself in other aspects of his life.

In a stress situation such as that resulting from the shipwreck and his subsequent experience on the raft, Mr Perdomo proved incapable of surviving alone, not only because of his injuries but also from a psychological standpoint. Far from giving his companion moral support at difficult moments, he persistently complained and played no part whatsoever in the survival effort. His main preoccupation following the shipwreck was the thought that he could have died, but although on occasions he thought of committing suicide it is highly unlikely that he would have put his thoughts into practice.

Mr Perdomo is an extrovert with an immature and unstable personality. He was always a highly strung person and this condition seems to have been accentuated to a certain extent following the shipwreck, but without at any time reaching such an extreme as to require psychiatric treatment.

The Machover test showed a considerable aggressiveness only partly repressed. There was also evidence of his extrovert tendencies, immaturity, lack of social adaptation, narcissism and insecurity.

SANTA CRUZ DE TENERIFE, 26 February, 1979
A. Garcia-Estrada Perez, Psychiatrist

Graphological Study of Epifanio's Personality

The little education Epifanio received had no effect on him whatsoever since, being devoid of spiritual feeling, he never assimilated what he learnt.

He is a common person and lacks good taste.

Although he has a marked tendency to associate with others, his gregariousness is misplaced and he quickly becomes too familiar and takes liberties, thus displaying a tactless and undiscerning nature.

Drawing the attention of others makes him feel important and compensates for his lack of self-assurance. When he thinks he can achieve distinction, particularly in the company of others regarded as inferior to himself, he immediately comes out with stories in which he assumes the leading role. His excessive fantasy, bordering on the Utopian, lacks a sense of reality, while a strong desire to impress others makes him talk garrulously, distorting facts, making things appear larger, exaggerating, complicating matters and presenting himself as the leading figure in any situation.

Emotionally immature, he behaves in a puerile manner. His lack of consideration towards others stems from his egoism and childishness.

His thinking process is also infantile, immature and underdeveloped. He has an excessive imagination, often exceeding the bounds of reason. He makes snap judgements without hardly ever working out the facts or attempting to distinguish right from wrong.

He has a very possessive and selfish nature, is extremely fond of money and has a generally high developed instinct of ownership. He is usually the first to make use of any collective advantage but the last to co-operate in a venture which does not appear to offer a specific reward, even where it does not call for a major effort.

His penchant for food, drink and other pleasures, including small-talk and time-wasting amusements, his inordinate desire to show off, his ostentation (vanity), gluttony and sexuality, to the point of over-indulgence, are all rooted in his immaturity and childishness. He likes to boast of what he believes to be his success in satisfying such pleasures.

Epifanio is not consciously in control of his emotions and his reactions are therefore unbalanced. Consequently he is impressionable, changeable, fickle and inconsistent. He changes friends as quickly as he changes his opinions and contradicts himself, according to the influence exerted by external situations on his unstable affectivity.

Applied to his behavioural pattern, this wavering affects his level of self-esteem. His mood can change quickly from a feeling of importance – a high level of self-esteem – to another where he feels frustrated – a low level of self-esteem.

He does very little and tends to prefer an idle, passive

existence. Any activity commenced is soon discontinued if it calls for a sustained effort. He avoids any responsibility, initiative or risk and is reluctant to pursue any idea or action which involves a voluntary sacrifice.

He displays a masochistic but relative aggressiveness – towards himself as an object of pity, but actually directed towards the lower family echelons – has a chauvinistic view of women, whom he regards solely as a means to derive pleasure, and lacks consideration for women in general and for his own wife in particular. He displays aggressiveness towards the members of his family by adopting a general attitude of indifference, not bothering about them save insofar as they can help satisfy his egoistic tendencies. Within the family circle he is irritable and is ever given to outbursts, stemming from a brusque and spasmodic sensory excitability (hysterical reactions).

He asserts his will in a capricious and childish manner, often behaving stubbornly and obstinately until he can satisfy his whims.

INTELLECTUAL CAPACITY

Has a childish, immature mind with under-developed powers of reasoning. His thoughts do not follow a logical or constructive pattern but are based on disconnected imagery. Lacks concentration and is given to day-dreaming. His excessive, uncontrolled imagination tends to be Utopian. Judgements highly subjective and inaccurate, only sees things as he wants to or as it suits him to see them. Lacks discernment.

Constantly changes his mind and contradicts himself. Attention good but mainly or almost exclusively directed towards experiences capable of satisfying his material needs.

Unable to pay close attention to tasks involving responsibility or a creative mental effort, but in manual jobs performed mechanically with virtually no human intervention, for which he is well-suited because of his high mental automatism, could achieve satisfactory performance.

MORAL STANDARDS

Epifanio's highly possessive and egoistic nature, fondness for money, lack of sincerity; the cunning way he achieves his selfish aims by hiding his feelings whenever it suits him or twisting facts and meanings; his lazy attitude and unwillingness to go out of his way to help others; his strong urge to experience personal sensation without making any attempt to control his instincts; his fickleness, irresponsibility are all factors which obviously add up to a low moral standard.

PSYCHIATRIC DIAGNOSIS AID

We are faced with a subject whose hysterical tendency induces him to live his desires as though they were reality. His excessively emotional nature – hyperemotionalism – which extends beyond his powers of control leads him to irrational and contradictory reactions depending on his level of self-esteem, which in turn is affected by his relations with others. Epifanio can adopt different and highly subjective attitudes according to whether he is in the company of inferiors or superiors. With the latter he assumes a conceited stance, boasts of his personal attributes, which he sees through an idealized imagination, and presents himself as the hero of his exploits, thus satisfying unexperienced desires which he describes and lives as though they were real, to the point where he almost enters into the realms of mythomania.

In a family situation – surrounded by inferiors – where he has no spectators, Epifanio's aggressiveness is displayed as irritability, violent attitudes and indifference towards the members of his family and also towards himself, in that he assumes the role of victim. The first manifestation is related or extended masochism, since his aggressive tendencies are a way of punishing himself for feeling inferior and are extended to the lower family echelons.

The second manifestation is masochism in the strictest sense, since the subject was labouring under frustration at the time the test was carried out. But because of his egoism or narcissism he could not let himself fall a victim to his own aggressive tendencies without deriving some benefit, so he unconsciously brought into operation a hysteroid defensive mechanism which made him appear before others as the victim of an exploit, and this partly offset his frustration.

When comparing the specimen written on the ship – prior to the disaster – with that written later, the first is seen to reflect an essentially narcissistic form of neurosis, an expression of vanity, a need for admiration, approval, esteem and affection from his superiors, together with a certain degree of instability and personality fulfilment.

In the second specimen, written by the subject in his own familiar surroundings, we encounter the inferiority complex, withdrawal and inhibitions caused by frustration. But at the same time it shows that his neurotic condition is less pronounced than it was seen to be prior to the shipwreck, that is conscious resources are good – his attentiveness, for instance – and that he is steadily developing towards an improved personality.

Given the existence of narcissistic neurosis or aurality,

which is a traumatic effect of the shipwreck and of the subject's present inability to adapt to reality, although he is making good progress, these guidelines may serve as a basis for applying suitable psychotherapy.

Given at Santa Cruz de Tenerife on the 10th day of February nineteen hundred and seventy nine.

Signed

CHAIRMAN OF THE CANARIAN-VENEZUELAN SOCIETY OF GRAPHOLOGY AND PSYCHOLOGY

Nor Iron Bars A Cage

Penelope Tremayne

'An inspiring example of how the human spirit can triumph over adversity'
Daily Mail

'Not only an exciting story, but a lasting achievement of great literary merit'
Patrick Leigh Fermor

In January 1986 Penelope Tremayne, an English woman in her sixties, was kidnapped by Tamil terrorists in Sri Lanka and held hostage for five weeks. *Nor Iron Bars A Cage* is the extraordinary account of that captivity – extraordinary not only because she endured and won through, but because of her unflinching determination to remain unbroken by her captors and to die honourably if she was to be shot. Together with her evocative recollections of her solitary travels in Greece as a young woman, written to maintain her morale during long days as a hostage, *Nor Iron Bars A Cage* is a compelling chronicle of self-discovery, intrepid adventure and great personal courage.

'A chilling, thrilling account of one plucky woman's determination to prove her point. It is also a thrilling inducement to travel, to *really* travel, to escape from ourselves, our petty lives, our burdensome artefacts and explore our marvellous planet'
Daily Mail

'Beautifully written. Her story is remarkable, and so is the book in which she tells it'
London Evening Standard

'There can be no doubt that this is a very brave woman'
Independent

Running the Gauntlet
The Battle for the Barents Sea

Frank Pearce
Foreword by Admiral of the Fleet Lord Lewin

Mercilessly tempestuous and icily cold, vital lifeline to beleaguered Russia and scene of the most poignant and dramatic battles in British naval history, the Barents Sea quickly became the axis around which revolved the crucial fight for dominance in World War Two.

It was here, in this 'Gateway to Hell' that the badly torpedoed *Edinburgh* made her last gallant stand but was sunk with five tons of gold bullion on board, here that Captain Sherbrooke's heroism vanquished the greatly superior foe, that, lurking in a nearby Norwegian fiord, the notorious German battleship, the mighty *Tirpitz*, was finally laid low, here that the tide of victory surged relentlessly on to force the collapse of Hitler's vicious Third Reich.

Drawing on first-hand accounts, on maps, original battle plans and his own years of service, Frank Pearce evokes in striking detail the feats of superhuman endurance, the loyalty, courage and fortitude of the Navy, running the gauntlet for British supremacy in the Barents Sea.

FONTANA PAPERBACKS

Malta Convoy

Shankland and Hunter

Only one tanker was fast enough to run the murderous Nazi blockade – the *Ohio*.

In 1942, a mighty convoy sailed to relieve the island of Malta. But lying in wait was a vast force of German submarines and aircraft...

One of the few survivors of that convoy was the SS *Ohio*. Here is the fantastic saga of the men who sailed her through every peril a relentless enemy could devise. When the *Ohio*, broken-backed and sinking, finally limped into Malta's harbour, she discharged from her straining holds the fate of the war itself.

'One of the classic sea stories of the war.' *Nicholas Monsarrat*

FONTANA PAPERBACKS